QUILTING HAPPINESS

PROJECTS, INSPIRATION, AND IDEAS TO MAKE QUILTING MORE JOYFUL

Christina Lane
and Diane Gilleland

POTTER
CRAFT

New York

Copyright © 2013 by Christina Lane and Diane Gilleland
Project photography copyright © 2013 by Potter Craft, an imprint of the Crown Publishing Group, a division of Random House, Inc.

All rights reserved.
Published in the United States by Potter Craft, an imprint of the Crown Publishing Group, a division of Random House, Inc., New York.
www.crownpublishing.com
www.pottercraft.com

POTTER CRAFT and colophon are registered trademarks of Random House, Inc.

Library of Congress Cataloging-in-Publication Data

Lane, Christina, 1980–
  Quilting happiness : projects, inspiration, and ideas to make quilting more joyful / by Christina Lane and Diane Gilleland.—First Edition.
    pages cm
1. Quilting—Patterns. I. Gilleland, Diane. II. Title.
  TT835.L329 2013
  746.46—dc23

2012047886

ISBN 978-0-7704-3409-0
eISBN 978-0-7704-3410-6

Printed in China

Illustrations by Christina Lane
Tools and Techniques photography by Sarah Costa

Project photographs by Heather Weston
Quilt journal image (page 18): Sarah Costa, Sarah Costa Photography
"Morning Seeing" image (page 19): Pam and Kirby Harris, Harris & Harris Photographics
"Inspiration Board" image (page 27): Hanna Andersson, ihanna.nu
"Blackbird Fly" quilt image (page 90, right): Krista Hennebury, poppyprints.blogspot.com
Diver quilt image (page 96): Kay Bailey, fiberofherbeing.blogspot.com
"do.Good Stitches" image (page 119): Nicke Cutler, kisskissquilt.blogspot.com
"Laid Back Ladies of the Block" image (page 134): Carol Porter
Cover photographs by Heather Weston except back cover, top, by Sarah Costa
Cover design by Laura Palese

10 9 8 7 6 5 4 3 2 1
First Edition

*For my mom, who taught me
this valuable lesson:
"You'll never notice it on a
galloping horse."*

—CHRISTINA

CONTENTS

INTRODUCTION

If you like to make quilts, then we have a big question for you. Which part of your latest project feels more valuable: the finished quilt itself, or the experiences you had while making it?

Let us introduce ourselves: Christina has been quilting since her high school years. Diane is a writer who only recently began dabbling in quilts. And our answer to the question above is: both the finished piece *and* the enjoyment of making it are equally valuable.

When we set out to write this book, we wanted to share a collection of beautiful quilt designs from Christina, but we also wanted to delve more deeply into why, exactly, quilting makes quilters so happy. When we make things, we're generally happy—whether we're creating with paints, plants, food, fabric, or any other medium. A creative state of mind is, after all, a positive state of mind. We get to delight in the colors and textures of our materials, and we get excited knowing that our hands are manifesting something that didn't exist before.

Quilting holds such rich possibilities for exploring the many joys of creativity. How, for example, can you add more meaning to your fabric choices? How does it feel to pour your heart into a quilt for a beloved friend? Do you find more joy in a curved seam sewn perfectly, or in a slightly wonky seam that nonetheless is uniquely your own? And what about sharing your passion with others? Would teaching friends to quilt give you a sense of satisfaction? What if you made projects for people in need in your hometown? And what about the worldwide community of quilters—might you find wonderful kindred spirits there?

What's interesting to both of us is that, while every quilter might derive happiness from quilting, the exact nature of that happiness will be different from person to person. For some, it's a welcome bit of solitude, while others use this craft to forge connection and community. Some find it in their design process. Some find it in curling up under the finished quilt, cup of tea in hand.

We hope this book will serve as a workbook of sorts to help you explore what makes you happiest in your quilting—and, just maybe, provide you with some fresh ideas to make your quilting hours even happier. We also hope this is a book you'll return to again and again, because it will spark different ideas on each rereading. You can use the creative exercises, practices, and journaling questions here throughout your quilting life, and you can reinterpret these projects in endless ways. We hope all of this boosts your love of quilting and brings you many hours of creative happiness.

Now, let's all go make something!

Christina Lane

Diane Gilleland

HOW TO USE THIS BOOK

We love traditional quilt block designs and we're intrigued by the modern quilt movement, so you'll find that these quilts adapt nicely to both traditional and modern fabrics.

This isn't quite a beginner's quilting book, although many of the projects in it are simple to make. We're assuming that you have a basic working knowledge of quilting, and that you know how to operate your sewing machine. Ideally, you'll already have some experience with handling and cutting fabrics.

If you need a refresher on a technique or are unfamiliar with a particular process, turn to Tools and Techniques (Chapter 5, page 147). This is also where you'll find instructions for the finishing steps that are common to every quilt project: making a backing, building a quilt sandwich, quilting, and binding. If you're pretty new to quilting, be sure to check out the Before You Begin page that follows for some helpful tips.

The projects in this book are broken into three skill levels:

 Advanced Beginner: These projects involve straight seams and simple construction.

 Intermediate: These projects involve some curved seams, or require a bit of careful seam matching and pinning.

 Experienced: These projects involve a lot of seam matching and precise construction.

That said, please don't feel too intimidated to try a project that seems to be at a higher skill level than you are. Try making one test block, or part of one row. You may find you're ready to take on more than you realize!

If the cutting instructions for these projects seem a little detailed to you, there's a good reason behind this. We've designed them so you don't have to figure out how you're supposed to get twenty-four pieces from that fat quarter; instead we'll explain how to cut your yardage into strips and then cut those strips down into pieces. (We'll use the term "subcut" as shorthand for this process; you can learn more about it on page 153.)

Throughout this book, you'll find happiness-related goodies: creative exercises, useful tools you can make, inspiring stories, questions to get you journaling, and practices to increase your enjoyment of quilting. Feel free to meander through these as you like, trying anything that appeals to you. Our guess is that each time you pull this book from your shelf, a different one of these happiness bits will catch your eye.

If you have a particularly nice quilting experience after you've read this book, or you have a finished quilt to show off, we'd love to see it and hear all about it! Please visit us at QuiltingHappiness.com. We'll provide the tea and cookies.

BEFORE YOU BEGIN

If you're new to quilting, here are some things to be aware of before you begin making the projects in this book.

- We recommend reading through all of the instructions for a project before you dive in. (And yes, we know how tempting it can be to just dive in!) It's especially important to read the instructions thoroughly before cutting fabrics or squaring quilt blocks.

- Most quilting cottons are 44/45" wide, so that's the width we've used to calculate yardage for most of the quilts in this book. (The Plus You Quilt and Cross-Stitch Quilt use 54"-wide fabrics.) When you shop for fabrics, check the bolts and make sure you're buying the correct width.

- The yardages in this book are calculated to make efficient use of your fabrics, with very little left over. If you're a new quilter, you might want to add about ½ yard to our yardages so you're covered in case there's a cutting error.

- These instructions are written for right-handed quilters; if you're left-handed, feel free to rotate pieces as needed so cutting feels more comfortable.

- To prepare your fabric for cutting, cut off the selvages and then square the yardage. Squaring makes your cutting much more accurate, and you can learn how on page 159.

- Quilt-piecing seams are always sewn with a ¼" seam allowance. If you haven't before, check to see if your sewing machine is making accurate ¼" seams. Page 154 tells you how.

- As you're assembling your quilts, pay special attention to matching seams; you'll find several helpful techniques on page 157.

- Many quilt projects reach a point at which you have lots of pieces to manage. It's much easier to assemble a quilt accurately if you keep your cut pieces and finished blocks stacked together. Sometimes it's helpful to pin paper labels to these stacks to help you keep track of their block or row numbers.

5 THINGS ABOUT QUILTING THAT MAKE US HAPPY

1. Using quilting as a break and an escape, a time to reflect and enjoy creating.
2. Creating something comforting, but useful as well.
3. Seeing how individual shapes create beautiful patterns.
4. The sense of accomplishment when a quilt is finished.
5. How meaningful it is to make something with my hands that will see generations of use.
   —CHRISTINA

1. Having an excuse to hoard beautiful fabrics.
2. Getting all my seams to line up on a particularly precise patchwork piece. This makes me dance in my sewing chair.
3. That sweet moment of snuggling into a handmade quilt.
4. How a quilt subtly ages over the years. The slight fade of colors, those little worn spots—they're a record of all the comfort I've enjoyed.
5. Give me some hand quilting to do, a cup of coffee, and a *Doctor Who* marathon, and I'm one happy woman.
   —DIANE

CHAPTER 1

INSPIRED *to* QUILT

The world is full of visual inspirations: the colors of your neighbor's flower garden, the pattern on that manhole cover you pass on your way to work, stacks of brilliant apples in the supermarket, the way the light hits your favorite vase in the morning. One of the great joys of quilting comes from transforming the things you see into masterpieces of cut-and-sewn fabric.

In this chapter, we'll explore some quilt projects that came from flashes of inspiration like these. We'll also get busy making playful tools to help you find and capture your own ideas. Each of us has our own "creative fingerprint"—a unique set of symbols, colors, textures, and ideas that sets our hearts to dancing, but also expresses who we are. Whether you're new to quilting or an old hand at it, we think it's always a good idea to explore your creative fingerprint and discover how it shows up in your work.

The ELEVATOR MUSIC QUILT

FINISHED BLOCK SIZE: THIS QUILT IS ASSEMBLED IN ROWS
RATHER THAN BLOCKS.
FINISHED QUILT SIZE: 54" X 68"

CHRISTINA: *"Sometimes I find quilt inspiration in the oddest places. Recently, I was watching the film* Public Enemies. *There was a scene with an elevator, and it had this interesting chain-link design on the doors. Luckily, I had my paper and pen handy, so I grabbed the remote, paused, and started sketching. That's how this quilt was born."*

DIANE: *"It really pays to have something to help capture those brainstorms as they happen, doesn't it? I have notebooks all over my house for just that reason."*

Skill Level:

PIECED BY HEATHER LOTT

SUPPLIES
Background: 2¼ yards white solid
Chain links: 1¼ yards green solid
Chain-link centers: 5 fat quarters, gray prints
Border: 8 fat quarters, assorted green prints
Backing: 3¼ yards your choice of fabric
Binding: ½ yard your choice of fabric
Batting: 58" × 72" (twin size)

FABRICS USED HERE
FreeSpirit Designer Solids: Arctic White and Lime
FreeSpirit: Various designer prints for border
Daisy Janie Organic Fabrics: Basic Gray by Jane DiCintio

CUTTING THE FABRICS

Background/White Solid:
Cut 3 strips, 6½" × width of fabric.
Subcut these as follows:
4 squares, each measuring 6½" × 6½"
4 lengths, each measuring 6½" × 8½"
4 lengths, each measuring 6½" × 10½"

Cut 19 strips, 2½" × width of fabric. Leave 3 strips uncut, and subcut 16 strips as follows:
10 lengths, each measuring 2½" × 18" (5 strips)
12 lengths, each measuring 2½" × 12½" (4 strips)
26 lengths, each measuring 2½" × 10½" (7 strips)
1 length measuring 2½" × 9½"
1 length measuring 2½" × 6"

Chain Links/Green Solid:
Cut 4 strips, 2½" × width of fabric. Do not subcut these.
Cut 2 strips, 6½" × width of fabric. Do not subcut these.
Cut 2 strips, 8½" × width of fabric. Subcut them into 18 lengths, each measuring 8½" × 2½".
Cut 2 pieces, each measuring 2½" × 9½", from the leftover fabric.
Cut 2 pieces, each measuring 6½" × 6", from the leftover fabric.

Chain-link Centers/Gray Prints:
Cut 1 strip, 6½" × 18", from each of the five gray prints.

Border/Green Prints:
Cut 2 strips, 2½" × 22", from each of the eight green prints.

ASSEMBLING THE QUILT BLOCKS

These aren't quilt blocks in the traditional sense. They are really individual units, which you'll combine later into rows to form the quilt top.

1. To begin, sew two $2\frac{1}{2}$" × width of fabric green strips to either side of one $2\frac{1}{2}$" × width of fabric white strip. Press the seam allowances toward the white strip. Square the left edge of this unit and then subcut it into six pieces, each measuring $6\frac{1}{2}$" × $6\frac{1}{2}$" **(Diagram A)**. These six pieces are Unit A.

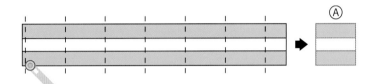

DIAGRAM A

2. Sew two $2\frac{1}{2}$" × width of fabric green strips to either side of one $2\frac{1}{2}$" × width of fabric white strip. Sew two $2\frac{1}{2}$" × $9\frac{1}{2}$" green strips to either side of one $2\frac{1}{2}$" × $9\frac{1}{2}$" white strip. Press the seam allowances of both units toward the white fabric. Square the left edges of both units and then subcut them into six pieces, each measuring $8\frac{1}{2}$" × $6\frac{1}{2}$" **(Diagram B)**. These six pieces are Unit B.

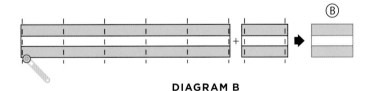

DIAGRAM B

3. Sew two $6\frac{1}{2}$" × width of fabric green strips to either side of one $2\frac{1}{2}$" × width of fabric white strip. Then, sew two $6\frac{1}{2}$" × 6" green strips to either side of one $2\frac{1}{2}$" × 6" white strip. Press the seam allowances toward the green fabric. Square the left edge of each unit and then subcut them into 18 pieces, each measuring $2\frac{1}{2}$" × $14\frac{1}{2}$" **(Diagram C)**. These 18 pieces are Unit C.

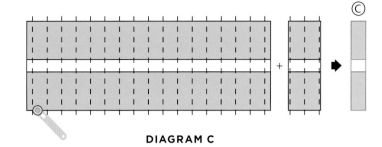

DIAGRAM C

4. Refer to **Diagram D** throughout this step. Sew two $2\frac{1}{2}$" × 18" white strips to either side of one $6\frac{1}{2}$" × 18" gray print strip. Repeat this process with the remaining gray print strips. Press the seam allowances toward the gray print strips and then square the left edge of each strip unit. From three of these strip units, subcut three pieces each, measuring $4\frac{1}{2}$" × $10\frac{1}{2}$". From the remaining two strip units, subcut two pieces each, measuring $4\frac{1}{2}$" × $10\frac{1}{2}$". You should have 13 pieces total.

   Next, sew a white $2\frac{1}{2}$" × $10\frac{1}{2}$" strip to the top and bottom edges of each of these units. Press the seam allowances toward the gray prints. These 13 units are Unit D. Set aside four of these units; you'll use them when you assemble the rows of this quilt.

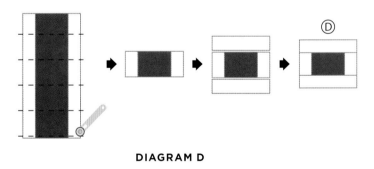

DIAGRAM D

5. Working with your nine remaining Unit Ds, orient them as shown in **Diagram E** and sew an $8^{1}/_{2}$" × $2^{1}/_{2}$" green strip to either side, pressing the seam allowances toward the green strips. Sew a Unit C to the top and bottom edges and press the seam allowances toward Unit C. These nine units are Unit E.

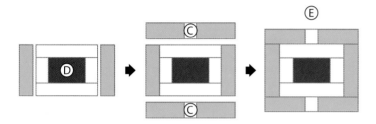

DIAGRAM E

6. To make the borders of the quilt, sew together eight $2^{1}/_{2}$" × 22" green print strips along their length, arranging the prints as you like. Press the seam allowances in alternating directions. Repeat this process with a second set of eight green print strips, arranging the prints in the same order. With the strips oriented horizontally, square the left edges of both units and then subcut them into 16 pieces, each measuring $2^{1}/_{2}$" × $16^{1}/_{2}$" **(Diagram F)**. These 16 pieces are Unit F.

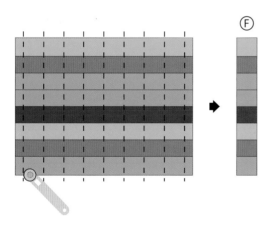

DIAGRAM F

Christina's Tips

- You'll be cutting a lot of different pieces of fabric with similar sizes for this quilt, and then working with many different pieced units. If you keep your stacks of pieces labeled, you'll save time.
- If you want to make this quilt border really scrappy, cut 118 squares from a lot of assorted fabrics, each measuring $2^{1}/_{2}$" × $2^{1}/_{2}$". Assemble them into two columns of 32 squares and two columns of 27 squares.

7. Sew four Unit Fs together end to end **(Diagram G)**. Make sure the colors repeat in the same order. The finished strip should contain 32 squares. Press the seam allowances to one side. Repeat this process with three more sets of Unit Fs, for a total of four border strips.

DIAGRAM G

ASSEMBLING THE QUILT TOP

8. To assemble Row 1, sew three Unit As, two $6^{1}/_{2}$" × $10^{1}/_{2}$" pieces, and two $6^{1}/_{2}$" × $6^{1}/_{2}$" pieces together, following **Diagram H** for placement. Press the seam allowances away from the Unit As. Repeat this process one more time to assemble Row 7.

| 6½" x 6½" | (A) | 6½" x 10½" | (A) | 6½" x 10½" | (A) | 6½" x 6½" |

DIAGRAM H

9. To assemble Row 2, sew together three Unit Es and four 2¹/₂" × 12¹/₂" pieces, following **Diagram I** for placement. Press the seam allowances toward the Unit Es. Repeat this process two more times to assemble Rows 4 and 6.

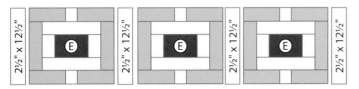

DIAGRAM I

10. To assemble Row 3, sew together three Unit Bs, two Unit Ds, and two 6¹/₂" × 8¹/₂" pieces, following **Diagram J** for placement. Press the seam allowances away from the Unit Bs. Repeat this process once more to assemble Row 5.

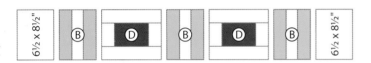

DIAGRAM J

11. You may want to lay your finished rows out at this point, using **Diagram K** for placement. Sew the rows together in order, pressing the seam allowances toward Rows 2, 4, and 6.

- -

Ideas for Quilting

- -

- Try outline quilting just outside each of the chains and inside the gray prints.
- If you're more adventurous, why not try a chain-link pattern across the width of the quilt top?
- A dense pattern of quilted leaves would be a nice complement to the greens in this quilt.

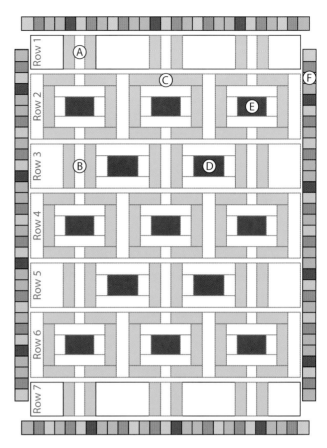

DIAGRAM K

12. Sew a 32-square border to the right and left edges of the quilt top, pressing the seam allowances toward the quilt top. Sew the remaining two borders to the top and bottom edges, matching the seam allowance of the first square in each border with the seam allowance of the side border. Trim away the excess squares after sewing, and press the seam allowances toward the quilt top.

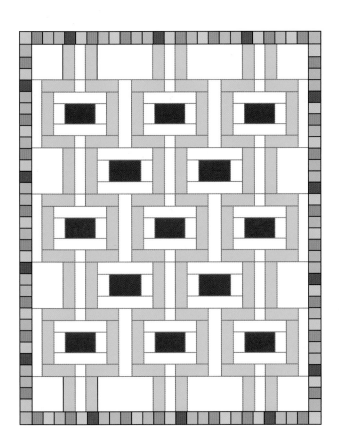

COMPLETED TOP

BACKING AND FINISHING

Make a 58" × 72" backing. Build a quilt sandwich and quilt. Cut seven 2" strips from your binding fabric and bind your quilt. (Refer to the Finishing Your Quilt section on page 159 as needed.)

Tools for Happiness:
MAKING YOUR QUILT JOURNAL

If you've been quilting for a while, you may already have a quilt journal. But if not, let's fix that right away! Find a blank book—one with high-quality paper and a cover that makes you smile. (Or, if that's too fancy, get an inexpensive spiral-bound notebook.) Write your name and the date on the first page and you're ready to begin.

A quilt journal is an all-important tool in your quilting practice. In it, you'll paste pictures and fabric swatches, jot down ideas, and make rough sketches of quilt patterns. You can also write about how colors affect you, or why a particular shape is captivating; your journal is a place for creative rumination. If possible, carry this journal with you everywhere, because any interesting object or idea you randomly encounter could become the foundation of your next quilt.

If you keep a quilt journal regularly, then over time you'll gradually grow a whole shelf of them, and they'll form a record of your growth as a quilter. You'll find it fascinating to page through glimpses of your earlier self. But a quilt journal isn't only about record keeping. It's about learning to listen to your artistic instincts. When your creative mind knows that you're capturing the brainstorms as they happen, something powerful takes place: you begin to have a lot more brainstorms!

This book you're reading, incidentally, contains a lot of interesting creative and thinking exercises. Your quilt journal would be a splendid space for playing with them!

Creative Exercise:

MORNING SEEING

Here's a seemingly simple practice that can reveal a lot about how you get inspired. First thing in the morning (well, you can get coffee first), get your quilt journal and jot down five things you see. Don't overthink the process; what five things do you notice first in your immediate environment? For example:

1. Your coffee mug this morning is your favorite one, with the yellow handle.
2. The tree outside your kitchen window is starting to lose some leaves.
3. The kitchen floor needs sweeping.
4. These blue placemats really glow in the morning sunlight.
5. The sun through that lace curtain is making an interesting shadow on the wall.

Don't give this list another thought; just put your journal away and go about your day. Keep this tiny practice up for thirty days, and then take a look at all your daily lists together. You should notice some patterns emerging.

Did you find yourself noticing the same objects and ideas very often? This is a sign you might need to vary your routines a little so your creative mind can have fresh input. Do the same shapes, colors, or objects pop up again and again? Maybe these are important

visual ideas or symbols for you, and perhaps they're begging to be incorporated into a new quilt. Do you tend to notice things that are fresh and dewy, or things that are interestingly dilapidated? What does this tell you about your visual style? Do you notice wildly different things every day? That's good information as well: Your tastes are eclectic, so perhaps there are interesting combinations you can make of seemingly unrelated ideas.

This exercise has one more subtle benefit: By training yourself to stop and notice your surroundings each morning, you're also learning to be a closer observer of your life. And that's always great fuel for new quilt design ideas!

The PLUS YOU QUILT

FINISHED BLOCK SIZE: 8½" X 8½"

FINISHED QUILT SIZE: 64" X 64"

DIANE: *"I love the linen used here! It contrasts so nicely with those traditional-looking prints."*

CHRISTINA: *"Linen is strong and wears well—it's been used in clothing for centuries. You don't see it in quilts all that much, so it's a breath of fresh air, especially paired with the very traditional calicos and primitive prints I chose here. I'm always inspired by old and new together."*

DIANE: *"That makes a good creativity prompt, too: pick out a fabric that represents your past, and then combine it with a fabric that represents your future. That would make for a quilt that tells your story in an interesting visual way."*

Skill Level:

SUPPLIES

Background: 2½ yards linen (54"-wide fabric)

Plus shapes: 6 fat quarters coordinating prints

Backing: 2 yards your choice of fabric

Binding: ½ yard your choice of fabric

Batting: 68" × 68" (twin size)

FABRICS USED HERE

Robert Kaufman: Antwerp Handkerchief Linen

Assorted vintage and reproduction prints from stash

CUTTING THE FABRICS

Background/Linen:

Cut 1 strip, 15½" × width of fabric.

Subcut it into 12 lengths, each measuring 2½" × 15½".

Cut 2 strips, 8½" × 64" from the length of the fabric (top and bottom borders).

Cut 2 strips, 8½" × 49" (side borders).

Cut 18 squares, each measuring 8½" × 8½", from remaining fabric.

Pluses/Prints (cut all pieces below from each print):

Cut 1 strip, 4½" × 15½"

Cut 3 pieces, each measuring 4½" × 8½"

Christina's Tips

- If you'd rather use a 44/45" quilting cotton instead of linen, the yardage you need is the same: 2½ yards. Just cut your border pieces first, and then make the other cuts listed in the cutting instructions.

- It's a good idea to prewash and dry your linen yardage so you can account for any shrinkage that might occur. Here's a great trick: remove the linen from the dryer while it's still slightly damp but almost dry, and then iron it right away. Ironing while it's slightly damp makes the job go much more quickly.

- Cotton batting is a good choice for a linen quilt because it's less likely to "beard," or work its way through the weave. Batting generally has a "right" and "wrong" side, so orient it per the manufacturer's instructions to help avoid bearding as well.

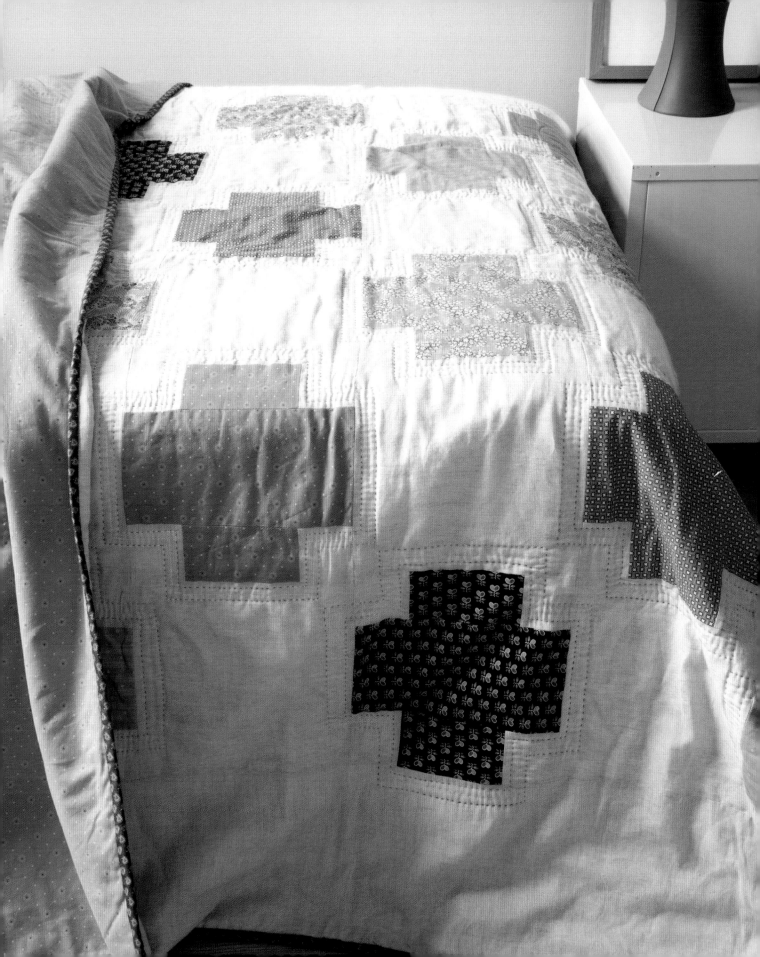

ASSEMBLING THE QUILT BLOCKS

1. Sew a $2^1/_2'' \times 15^1/_2''$ linen strip to either side of a $4^1/_2'' \times 15^1/_2''$ strip of print fabric, and press the seam allowances open. Square one end of this unit and subcut it into six pieces, each measuring $2^1/_2'' \times 8^1/_2''$ **(Diagram A)**.

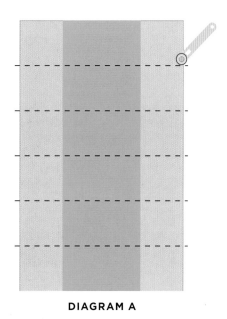

DIAGRAM A

2. Sew two of these units to a matching $4^1/_2'' \times 8^1/_2''$ print strip and press the seam allowances open **(Diagram B)**. Your finished block should measure $8^1/_2'' \times 8^1/_2''$.

3. Repeat Steps 1 and 2 with the remaining prints. You should have three blocks of each print, for a total of 18 blocks.

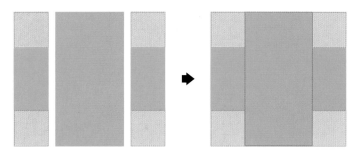

DIAGRAM B

ASSEMBLING THE QUILT TOP

4. You might find it helpful at this point to designate your six print fabrics as Print A through Print F. Use these designations and **Diagram C** to lay your blocks out and arrange the prints evenly. Sew each row of squares together, orienting the long center strip of the plus blocks in the same direction. Press the seam allowances open.

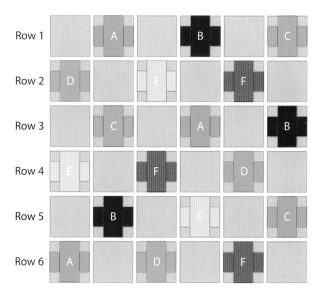

DIAGRAM C

5. Sew the finished rows together, pressing the seam allowances open.

6. Sew an $8^1/_2'' \times 49''$ border to the right and left edges of the quilt, and press the seam allowances open. Trim any excess fabric from the top and bottom edges of the borders.

7. Sew an $8^1/_2'' \times 64''$ border to the top and bottom edges of the quilt, pressing the seam allowances open **(Diagram D)**.

BACKING AND FINISHING

Make a 68″ × 68″ backing. Build a quilt sandwich and quilt. Cut seven 2″ strips from your binding fabric and bind your quilt. (Refer to the Finishing Your Quilt section on page 159 as needed.)

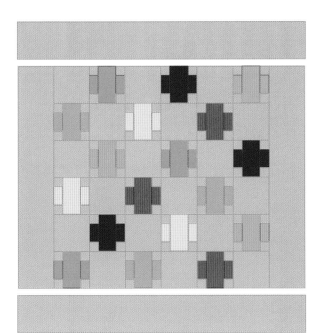

DIAGRAM D

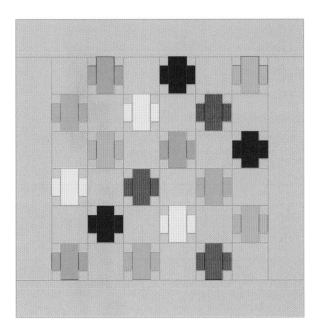

COMPLETED TOP

Ideas for Quilting

- Hand quilt with a bold running stitch around each of the plus shapes, echoing the shape a few times and blending one block into the next.
- For a simpler approach, stitch horizontal and vertical lines across the rows and down the columns.
- This would be a great quilt for tie quilting (see page 163).

Creative Exercise: **FABRIC PLAY**

We've suggested creative exercises involving seeing and sketching so far, but we never underestimate the importance of simply messing about with fabric scraps.

Here's an interesting way to find new inspiration: pull six fabric scraps out of your stash. Don't worry too much about them matching; just grab the first pieces that jump out at you. Cut them into roughly equal strips and put the strips into a paper bag or box.

Then, pull out two strips at a time and sew them together in pairs. Arrange and rearrange them until you arrive at a pleasing combination. Maybe you'll cut them into smaller pieces, or maybe you'll add a background. Once you have a configuration you like, sew it together.

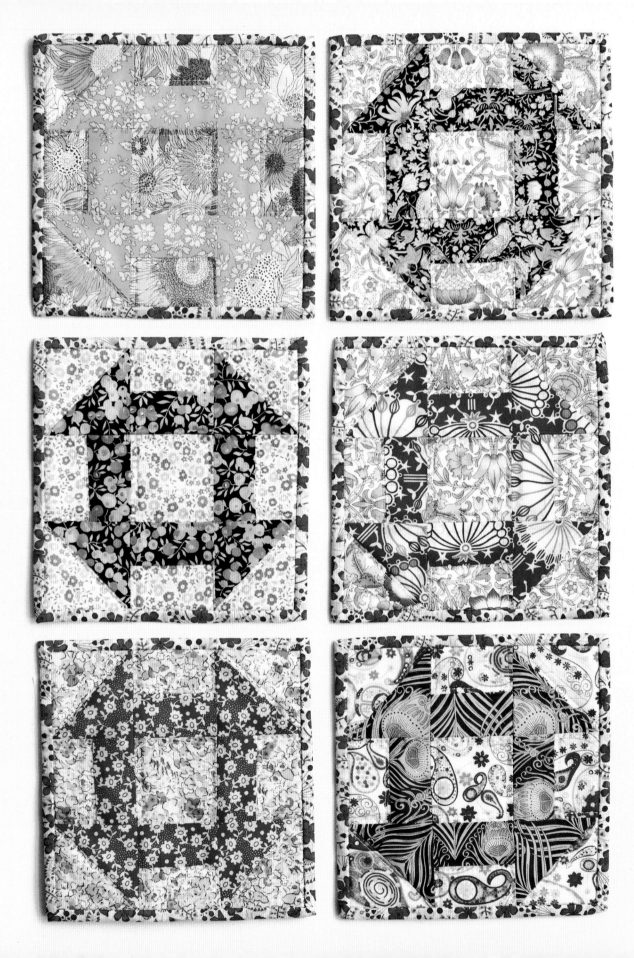

The LIBERTY MINI-QUILT ART

FINISHED BLOCK SIZE: 6½" X 6½"

DIANE: *"This is a nice way to add some quilted warmth to a space without making an entire quilt."*

CHRISTINA: *"I actually arrived at this project while I was making a quilt! I had a stash of print fabrics, and was trying to decide which color combinations worked best. So I made several blocks and pinned them to my studio wall. Usually, after a few days of this 'audition' process, a clear winner emerges, but in this case, I still liked them all. And I loved how they looked hanging on the wall."*

DIANE: *"I like the flexibility of this idea. I have a very small wall space in my office that would hold just three of these blocks perfectly. Or, I could see them stretched out in a horizontal row over my sofa."*

Skill Level:

SUPPLIES (PER BLOCK)

Block: 2 coordinating fat eighths, one light value and one dark value

Backing: 1 fat eighth your choice of fabric

Binding: 2" × 36" your choice of fabric

Batting: 7½" × 7½"

Hanging: ¼" dowel, cut to 5¾" length; or 2 flat-head thumbtacks

FABRICS USED HERE

Liberty of London: Tana Lawn

CUTTING THE FABRICS

Fabric A (darker fabric):
Cut 1 square, 4¼" × 4¼"
Cut 1 strip, 1½" × 10"

Fabric B (lighter/background fabric):
Cut 1 square, 4¼" × 4¼"
Cut 1 strip, 1½" × 10"
Cut 1 square, 2½" × 2½"

ASSEMBLING THE BLOCK

1. Working with the 4¼" squares from Fabric A and Fabric B, assemble four half square triangles. Square each one to 2½" × 2½" (see page 155).

2. Sew the 10" strips of Fabric A and Fabric B together along their length. Press the seam allowance open. Cut this unit into four squares, each measuring 2½" × 2½" **(Diagram A)**.

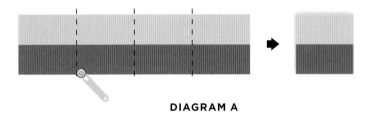

DIAGRAM A

3. Assemble the three rows of the block, using **Diagram B** for placement and orientation. Press all seam allowances open.

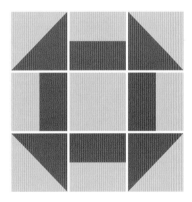

DIAGRAM B

4. Sew the rows together and press the seam allowances open. Square this block to 6½" × 6½" (see page 159).

5. Cut a 7½" × 7½" square from your backing fabric. Layer the backing, batting, and block, and quilt them. (The sample blocks are quilted along the inside edge of their patchwork pattern.) Repeat Steps 1 through 5 for each additional block.

FINISHING

6. To make this mini-quilt easy to hang, cut two 2½" squares of fabric from scraps, and fold them in half diagonally **(Diagram C)**. Press the folds.

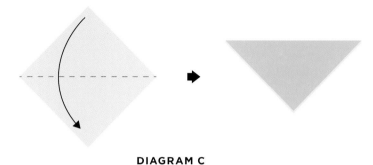

DIAGRAM C

7. Pin these triangles to the back of the mini-quilt, lining the raw edges up with the top and sides of the block **(Diagram D)**.

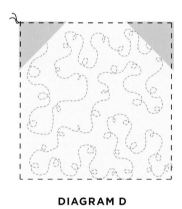

DIAGRAM D

8. Bind the block (see page 165). Be sure to catch the edges of both triangles in your stitching as you attach the binding.

9. To hang your mini-quilt, slide a dowel into the triangle pockets on the back and hang the quilt on a nail. Or, slide a flat-head thumbtack into each triangle pocket, pushing the sharp points out through the pocket fabric. Tack your mini-quilt to a wall and the tacks won't show.

If you're a creative person, an inspiration board is one of the best gifts you can give yourself. There's nothing to it! Just buy a pretty bulletin board at the home-goods store, or mount some cork squares on a wall. Then get yourself some push pins and you're ready to get started.

In its simplest form, an inspiration board is a place to tack up images and objects that appeal to you. These can be anything: scraps of wallpaper, pages torn from magazines, photographs, ticket stubs, fabric swatches, strands of yarn, interesting packaging labels, and so on. But if all you do is pin things up, then your inspiration board can quickly become more cluttered than inspiring. The best way to use an inspiration board is to tend it like a visual garden.

There are a million ways to approach this tending, so experiment and see what feels most creatively nourishing to you. Maybe you'll want to pin up only images that relate to your current quilt-in-progress, and then take them all down when you finish it. Maybe you'll want to set aside time once or twice a month to rearrange your inspiration board like a big collage, adding new bits and removing things you've grown tired of, and see what new visual ideas emerge from that process. Maybe you'll want to use your board as a kind of visual timeline, pinning items to it for a week, photographing the result, and then taking everything down to start fresh the next week. Or maybe you'll want to create some little sections on your board and have separate groupings of objects that appeal to you.

However you approach it, think of your inspiration board as a cross between a visual candy store and an incubator. It can be a source of great delight, and each time you glance at it, you're making new associations and hatching new ideas.

The CROSS-STITCH QUILT

FINISHED BLOCK SIZE: 10½" X 10½"

FINISHED QUILT SIZE: 50" X 60"

CHRISTINA: *"This is the softest quilt ever! I made it from voile, which is a very light, slightly sheer cotton. Voile is a little more challenging to work with than quilting cotton, but this was part of what drew me to it in the first place—it's a step outside my creative comfort zone. And did I mention it was soft?"*

DIANE: *"I love the way you combined a print background with all those print 'crosses,' too. The whole thing has a warmth to it that goes nicely with that softness."*

Skill Level:

SUPPLIES

Yardage for the top, backing, and binding of this quilt is figured for 54"-wide voile. If you prefer to make this design from quilting cottons instead, see below for adjusted yardages.

Background: 3 yards print

Crosses: ¼ yard each of 4 pink prints, light to dark values

Crosses: ¼ yard each of 4 blue prints, light to dark values

Backing: 1⅞ yards your choice of fabric

Binding: ½ yard your choice of fabric

Batting: 54" × 64" (twin size)

FABRICS USED HERE

FreeSpirit Fabrics: Little Folks Voile by Anna Maria Horner

CUTTING THE FABRICS

Background/Print:

Cut 9 strips, 7" × width of fabric. (If you're using 44/45" fabric, cut 12 strips.)

Subcut them into 60 squares, each measuring 7" × 7". Cut each of these squares in half on the diagonal, for a total of 120 half-square triangles.

Cut 2 strips, 2" × width of fabric. Subcut them into 30 squares, each measuring 2" × 2".

Cut 7 strips, 3" × width of fabric. Subcut 6 strips to 3" × 32½" and 1 strip to 3" × 24½".

Cut 7 strips, 2" × width of fabric. Subcut 6 strips to 2" × 32½" and 1 strip to 2" × 24½".

Crosses/Prints:

From 3 pink prints and 3 blue prints, cut 2 strips each, 2" × width of fabric.

Subcut these to 2" × 32½".

From the remaining pink and blue prints, cut 2 strips each, 2" × width of fabric.

Subcut these to 2" × 24½".

Yardage for 44/45"-Wide Fabrics:

Background: 3½ yards

Crosses: ¼ yard each of 8 prints

Backing: 3 yards

Binding: ½ yard

ASSEMBLING THE QUILT BLOCKS

1. Follow **Diagram A** for this step. Sew a 2" × 32¹/₂" cross strip to a 2" × 32¹/₂" background strip. Sew a second 2" × 32¹/₂" cross strip of the same print to the background strip. Then sew a 3" × 32¹/₂" background strip to the cross strip. Press the seam allowances toward the cross fabric strips. With the strips oriented horizontally, square the left edge of this unit and then subcut it into 16 pieces, each measuring 2" × 7¹/₂". Repeat this process with the rest of the pink and blue 32¹/₂" strips to create 96 units.

2. Repeat Step 1 with the 24¹/₂" strips, creating one pink unit and one blue one. Square the edge of each unit and subcut it into 12 pieces, each measuring 2" × 7¹/₂". You should have 24 units.

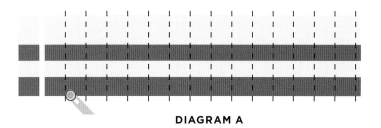

DIAGRAM A

3. Use **Diagram B** for Steps 3 through 5. Assemble each block using four units from Steps 1 and 2 (all four strips should be the same fabric). Begin by sewing two strips to opposite sides of a 2" background square. Press the seam allowances toward the cross fabric.

4. Next, take the other two strip units and sew a background triangle to either side. The background ends of the strips will stick out beyond the triangles, but you'll deal with that when you square the blocks. Press the seam allowances toward the strips.

5. Pin the corner units from Step 4 to either side of the long strip created in Step 3. Nestle the seam allowances of the cross squares with the back-ground piece in the center of the long strip (see page 157 for more on nestling). Sew the pieces together, pressing the seam allowances toward the center strip.

Christina's Tips

- Voile's softness and drape can make the pieces shift as you're sewing. If you're new to voile, you might find it easier to work with if you treat it with spray starch before you sew.
- You might find piecing voile easier if you switch to a walking foot on your sewing machine. You may need to adjust your machine's tension as well (see page 154).
- Wash your voile quilt on a delicate cycle in cold water. It's best to dry voile by hanging it or laying it flat, but you can also use an air-only cycle in your dryer. Or, partially dry your quilt on very low heat, and then hang it or lay it flat to finish drying. If your voile happens to get a stain, make a baking soda or borax paste and apply it to the stain for an hour, then wash.
- You'll find a 12½" square ruler handy for squaring the quilt blocks.

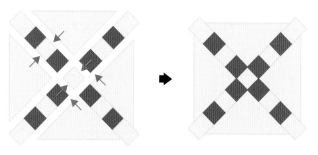

DIAGRAM B

6. Repeat Steps 1 through 5 with all eight prints to make a total of 30 quilt blocks.

7. Square these blocks to 10½″ × 10½″, using the process below so that the seams at the top and bottom of the finished blocks line up perfectly.

   Place a block on your cutting surface, oriented with the center strip running from bottom left to top right, as shown in **Diagram C**. Lay your ruler on top, lining up the 5¼″ measurement lines on the top and right edges of the ruler with the center of the block (see page 154 for more information on finding centers). Also, make sure that the diagonal line on your ruler is running through the center of the diagonal strip. Trim the right and top edges of the block. Then, turn the block 180 degrees and trim it to 10½″ × 10½″.

   Repeat this process to square the remaining blocks, making sure you orient them all the same way before trimming them.

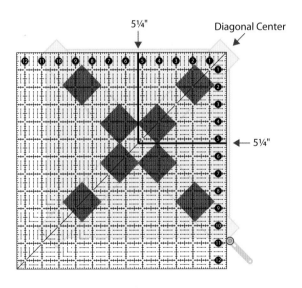

5¼″

Diagonal Center

5¼″

DIAGRAM C

ASSEMBLING THE QUILT TOP

8. Designate your prints as Pink 1 through 4 and Blue 1 through 4, and lay your quilt blocks out in six rows of five blocks each, following **Diagram D**.

9. Sew the blocks of Row 1 together. Be careful to nestle the seams in the corners of each block. Press the seam allowances to one side, in the same direction. Repeat this process to assemble five more rows, alternating the direction you press the seam allowances for each row.

10. Sew Rows 1 through 3 together into one section, and then sew Rows 4 through 6 together in a separate section. Sew the two sections together and press all seam allowances open.

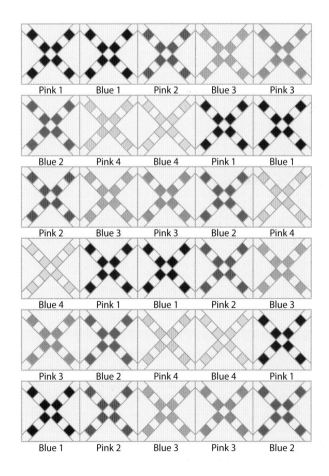

Pink 1	Blue 1	Pink 2	Blue 3	Pink 3
Blue 2	Pink 4	Blue 4	Pink 1	Blue 1
Pink 2	Blue 3	Pink 3	Blue 2	Pink 4
Blue 4	Pink 1	Blue 1	Pink 2	Blue 3
Pink 3	Blue 2	Pink 4	Blue 4	Pink 1
Blue 1	Pink 2	Blue 3	Pink 3	Blue 2

DIAGRAM D

COMPLETED TOP

BACKING AND FINISHING

Make a 54" × 64" backing. Build a quilt sandwich and quilt. Cut six 2" strips from your binding fabric and bind your quilt. (Refer to the Finishing Your Quilt section on page 159 as needed.)

Ideas for Quilting

- This soft fabric is beautifully complemented with an allover pattern of feather quilting.
- Stippling would also work nicely.
- For a simpler option, try stitching in straight lines, echoing the "X" shapes of the blocks and covering the entire top to create a nice texture.

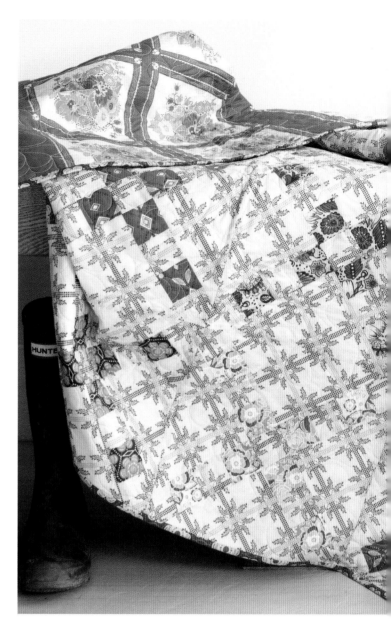

Can you name a quilter whose work you particularly admire? Maybe it's someone you've seen in a magazine or on TV, or maybe it's a favorite quilt blogger or one of your quilter friends. You can actually cultivate a lot of inspiration by looking closely at the work of this quilter—not to copy what that person does, but to analyze how it is done.

Try this exercise: Choose one quilter you admire (and you should have access to a lot of photographs of her quilts). Gather at least ten images of this quilter's work together in front of you. You can work on a computer, pulling images from websites, or with printed photographs and magazine pages. Now, grab your quilt journal and answer some questions:

What themes do you see in these quilts?

What colors show up again and again?

What shapes do you see frequently?

Do the quilts have a larger or smaller scale to their patterns?

Are they more abstract or more representational?

Are the fabrics bold, subdued, brightly colored, or neutral?

What would you say is this quilter's signature technique?

What techniques does she do well that you haven't learned yet?

What you're doing here is decoding this quilter's style and approach to the craft. The things you notice most will give you some important clues as to the visual ideas and techniques you might want to explore. Again, this isn't about copying; it's about finding new inspiration to help you take your quilting in fresh directions.

The CAN'T HELP MYSELF QUILT

FINISHED BLOCK SIZE: 15½" X 15½"

FINISHED QUILT SIZE: 45" X 60"

CHRISTINA: *"I named this quilt in honor of an intense creative period I had about a year ago, when I was inspired with a whole slew of quilt designs at the same time. There were so many, I literally couldn't help but design quilts!"*

DIANE: *"I love those times when you're in the grip of creating and the ideas are flowing. I wish I could stay in that state all the time, but then again, I know the creative mind also needs periods of rest."*

CHRISTINA: *"That's true! Right after that burst, I didn't design anything for a couple weeks. But I try to enjoy both the quiet moments and the crazily productive ones."*

Skill Level:

SUPPLIES

Background: 2¼ yards gray solid
Center Square: 1 fat quarter print
Small Triangle #1 and #3: 2 fat
    quarters coordinating prints
Small Triangle #2: ½ yard of a third
    coordinating print
Flying Geese: ½ yard each of
    2 coordinating prints
Backing: 2¾ yards your choice of
    fabric
Binding: ½ yard your choice of
    fabric
Batting: 49" × 64" (twin size)

FABRICS USED HERE

FreeSpirit Fabrics: Good Folks by
    Anna Maria Horner
FreeSpirit Fabrics: Designer Solids
    in Manatee

CUTTING THE FABRICS

Background/Gray Solid:
Cut 5 strips, 8" × width of fabric.
Subcut them into 24 squares, each
    measuring 8" × 8".
Cut 2 strips, 5¼" × width of fabric.
Subcut them into 12 squares,
    each measuring 5¼" × 5¼". Cut
    each square on both diagonals,
    creating a total of 48 quarter
    square triangles.
Cut 6 strips, 5" × width of fabric.
Subcut them into 48 squares, each
    measuring 5" × 5".

Center Square Print:
Cut 3 strips, 4" × 22".
Subcut them into 12 squares, each
    measuring 4" × 4".

Small Triangle #1:
Cut 3 strips, 5" × 22".
Subcut them into 12 squares, each
    measuring 5" × 5".

Small Triangle #2:
Cut 3 strips, 5" × width of fabric.
Subcut them into 24 squares, each
    measuring 5" × 5".

Small Triangle #3:
Cut 3 strips, 5" × 22".
Subcut them into 12 squares, each
    measuring 5" × 5".

Flying Geese #1:
Cut 2 strips, 6½" × width of fabric.
Subcut them into 12 squares, each
    measuring 6½" × 6½".

Flying Geese #2:
Cut 2 strips, 6½" × width of fabric.
Subcut them into 12 squares, each
    measuring 6½" × 6½".

ASSEMBLING THE QUILT BLOCKS

Each block is actually a combination of three different units, which you'll assemble individually and then sew together to form the final quilt block.

CENTER SQUARE UNIT

1. Sew two gray background triangles to opposite sides of a center square **(Diagram A)**. Center the pieces before stitching (see page 154 for more on centering). Press the seam allowances toward the background fabric.

2. Sew gray triangles to the other two edges of the square, again centering the pieces before sewing. Press the seam allowances toward the print.

3. Repeat Steps 1 and 2 with the remaining center squares for a total of 12 center square units. Square them to 5½″ × 5½″ (see page 159).

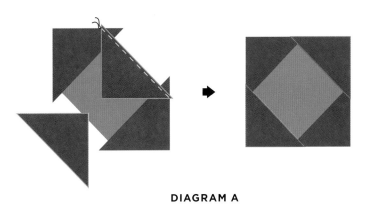

DIAGRAM A

HALF SQUARE TRIANGLES UNIT

We'll refer to Half Square Triangles as HSTs. For details on how to assemble HSTs, see page 155. We'll also be referring to the three print fabrics in these units as pink (Small Triangle Print #1), green (Small Triangle Print #2), and blue (Small Triangle Print #3).

4. Use the 5″ print squares and 5″ background solid squares to create 96 HSTs from the green print, 48 HSTs from the pink print, and 48 HSTs from the blue print. Square each of these units to 3″ × 3″.

5. Sew a pink HST to a green HST, orienting them as you see in **Diagram B**. Press the seam allowance toward the pink print. Now, sew a green HST to a blue HST. Press the seam allowance toward the blue print.

6. Sew these two units together **(Diagram B)**. Press the seam allowance toward the green and blue HSTs. Repeat this process with the rest of the HSTs to create a total of 48 units.

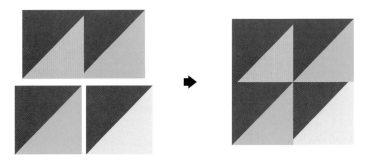

DIAGRAM B

FLYING GEESE UNIT

To simplify these instructions, we'll refer to the two print fabrics in these units as orange (Flying Geese Print #1) and dark pink (Flying Geese Print #2).

7. Center a 6½″ print square (either color) on top of an 8″ background square with right sides facing. With an erasable marking tool, draw a diagonal line down the center of both pieces **(Diagram C)**. Pin the pieces together, and then stitch ¼″ to each side of that line. Cut the fabric on the line, open the

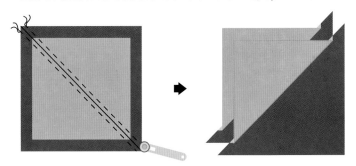

DIAGRAM C

resulting units flat, and press the seam allowances toward the print fabric, creating two squares.

8. Lay one square on top of the other with right sides facing. Orient the print triangles so they're at opposite corners **(Diagram D)**. Line up the edges of the squares, *not the seams*. Now, draw a diagonal line down the center again, orienting it as shown in **Diagram D**. Pin the squares together and stitch ¼" to each side of that line. Cut the fabric on the line and then carefully clip into the seam allowance halfway along the seam (page 158). Press the seam allowances toward the prints.

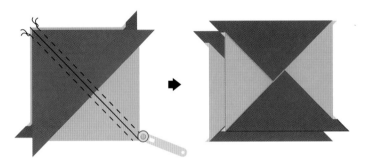

DIAGRAM D

9. Cut each of these squares in half. Place a ruler over one square, measuring ¼" from the point of one of the triangles, as shown in **Diagram E**. Cut the square. Then, turn the other half of the square 180 degrees, place your ruler over it, and trim it to ¼" from the point.

Christina's Tips

- This quilt contains a lot of seam allowances, which can become bulky. Follow the pressing instructions carefully to minimize bulk.
- For this pattern, you'll need to mark your fabric as you assemble some of the blocks. We recommend using a FriXion pen, which erases with the heat of your iron (page 149).

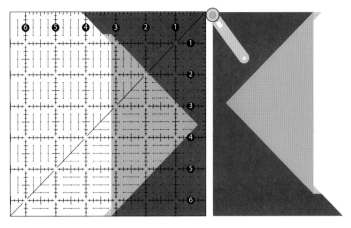

DIAGRAM E

Repeat this process with the second double triangle unit, making a total of four flying geese units.

10. To square the flying geese units, orient a unit with its triangle point facing left. Lay your ruler over the unit, lining the 3" measurement line up with the left edge of the unit. Trim the right edge of the triangle. Now, move your ruler until the 5½" measurement is at the bottom tip of the triangle **(Diagram F)**. Make sure the top of the ruler lines up with the upper point of the triangle. Trim the top edge of the unit. Now rotate the block 180 degrees and square the block to 5½" long. The top of your ruler should line up with the other point of the triangle. Your finished unit should measure 3" × 5½", with ¼" of background fabric beyond the point of the triangle.

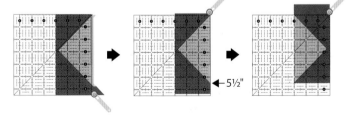

←5½"

DIAGRAM F

11. Repeat Steps 7 through 10 with the remaining flying geese units, making a total of 48 flying geese of each print.

12. Sew one orange unit to one dark pink unit, orienting them as shown in **Diagram G**. Be careful that your seam doesn't cut off the point of the lower triangle. Press the seam allowance toward the upper triangle. Repeat this process with the rest of the flying geese, making a total of 24 units.

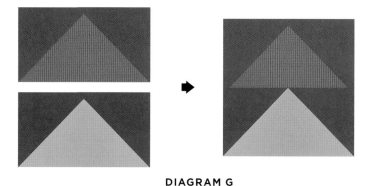

DIAGRAM G

DIAGRAM H

FINAL QUILT BLOCK

It's best to assemble the units into rows and then sew them together. Use **Diagram H** for placement and orientation.

13. Sew an HST unit to either side of a flying geese unit. Press the seam allowances toward the flying geese. Repeat this process to create a total of 24 rows, which are the top and bottom rows of the final blocks.

14. Sew a flying geese unit to either side of a center square unit. Press the seam allowances toward the flying geese. Repeat this process to create a total of 12 rows, which are center rows of the final blocks. As you assemble these rows, be sure to orient your center square the same way each time.

15. Sew a top row to a center row, nestling all the seams of the base units together (see page 157). Sew a bottom row to the center row, nestling the seams again. Press both seam allowances in the same direction.

16. Repeat Steps 13 through 15 to assemble a total of 12 blocks.

COMPLETED BLOCK

ASSEMBLING THE QUILT TOP

17. Place the first two blocks of Row 1 together, orienting them so their row seam allowances are lying in opposite directions. Nestle the row seams and sew them together, pressing the seam allowance open. Repeat this process to add a third block to Row 1.

18. Repeat Step 17 to assemble three more rows.

19. Sew Rows 1 and 2 together, matching the open seams (see page 157). Repeat this process to sew Rows 3 and 4 together.

20. Sew the two completed sections together, matching all seams. Press all seam allowances open.

COMPLETED TOP

BACKING AND FINISHING

Make a 46" × 64" backing. Build a quilt sandwich and quilt. Cut six 2" strips from your binding fabric and bind your quilt. (Refer to the Finishing Your Quilt section on page 159 as needed.)

Ideas for Quilting

- The sample quilt is quilted with a feathered wreath in each of the blocks and swirls filling in the surrounding spaces (see photo on page 10). This method adds a lot of subtle texture to a visually stimulating quilt.
- If feathers aren't your thing, try using all the interconnected squares in this quilt as a basis for quilting. Quilt around the edges of each square shape you can see. These squares will interconnect to form a pattern of their own.
- Stippling is always a nice choice on a busy quilt like this one, as are allover swirls.

Answer This:

Take out your quilting journal and ponder these questions.

- What does inspiration feel like to you? Is it a flash in your mind, a quickening of your pulse? Something else?
- Where does inspiration tend to visit you most? In your quilting space? While exercising outdoors? While reading or traveling or watching TV?
- How often are you inspired? Do you get small ideas often, or great big ideas at longer intervals?

CHAPTER 2

QUILTING *for* YOURSELF

Every quilter is on a unique path. Some of us are careful measurers and precise stitchers. Some of us are looser and more improvisational. Some of us like intricacy, some like simplicity, and on and on. Quilting is more than following patterns. It's a lifelong process of making design decisions, practicing techniques, and creating quilt after quilt. And together, those quilts reflect not only the timeline of your life, but the path that led you deeper into the craft.

In this chapter, we'll look at how quilting is an expression of you, and what it gives to you. You'll get to know yourself as a quilter a little better, and we hope you'll find some interesting creative exercises to help you experience your quilting hours more deeply. We'll also share some quilt projects that are eager to take on your unique creative touches.

The CRAZY STRIPS QUILT

FINISHED BLOCK SIZE: THIS QUILT IS ASSEMBLED IN STRIPS
RATHER THAN BLOCKS.
FINISHED QUILT SIZE: 46" X 58"

DIANE: *"I'm such a measure-phobic quilter, this improvisational piecing really appeals to me."*

CHRISTINA: *"I'd call it 'somewhat improv.' To me, improvisational piecing means starting with no direction or specific cuts, and in this quilt we do start with some loosely measured pieces. I'm a fan of precision and having steps to follow that lead to exact results every time. So this quilt represents me stepping outside my creative comfort zone."*

DIANE: *"I see what you mean, and I like how, even though the angles in the piecing are variable, there's an overall structure in those three wide strips. Further proof that good things can happen outside those comfort zones!"*

Skill Level:

SUPPLIES
Fabric A: 1½ yards solid
Fabric B: 1½ yards solid
Backing: 2⅞ yards your choice of fabric
Binding: ½ yard your choice of fabric
Batting: 50" × 62" (twin size)

FABRICS USED HERE
Oakshott Fabrics: Colourshott 47 Thistle
Oakshott Fabrics: Elements Earth 29 Quicksilver

CUTTING THE FABRICS
Fabric A: Cut 3 strips, 15½" × width of fabric.
Subcut them into various widths (see Note below).
Fabric B: Cut 3 strips, 15½" × width of fabric.
Subcut them into various widths (see Note below).
Note: You get to decide how wide to cut your fabrics—that's part of the improvisational nature of this quilt. The sample quilt contains strips measuring 2½", 3½", 5½", and 7½" wide, with most of them being 3½" and 5½" widths. If you want to piece this top faster, you can always cut fewer pieces and use wider widths.

Christina's Tips

- You'll find a 6" × 24" ruler very handy for this project, since you'll be making a lot of very long cuts.

ASSEMBLING THE QUILT STRIPS

1. Begin your first strip with a wider piece of Fabric A. Place it on your cutting mat right side up **(Diagram A)**. Place your ruler at the right edge of the fabric, and position it at an angle you like. (Diagram A provides one example, but feel free to experiment.) It's a good idea for the overall quilt design to keep your angle noticeable, but not too drastic. Cut the fabric with your rotary cutter.

2. Leave this first strip on your cutting mat and grab a strip of Fabric B (for the sake of illustration, we'll say a moderate sized piece, maybe 5½″ wide). Slide this second piece of fabric slightly under your first piece, until they are just overlapping at the longest edge as shown in **Diagram B**. Lay your ruler along the original diagonal cut you made in Step 1, and trim Fabric B to match. Discard the excess of Fabric B.

3. Line up the cut edges of these two pieces as shown in **Diagram C**. Sew them together and press the seam allowance toward Fabric B. Take this unit back to your cutting mat.

4. Now, you'll make another angled edge, this time by cutting both fabrics at once. Place your finished unit from Step 3 on your cutting mat **(Diagram D)**. Choose another Fabric A piece in a width you like and place it under Fabric B. Place your ruler over both pieces of fabric, orienting it at an angle you like, and cut. Discard the excess from both fabrics.

5. Match up the raw edges as shown in **Diagram E** and sew this piece to the strip. Press the seam allowance toward Fabric A. Repeat this process to continue adding new pieces to the strip, alternating fabrics as you go. Press each seam allowance toward the newest piece on the strip.

As you're piecing, vary your fabric widths and cutting angles for visual interest—and every once in a while, reverse the cutting angle for variety. As you add each new piece, think about how deep

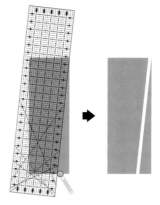
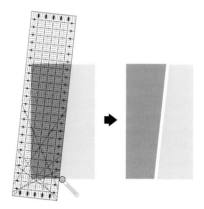

DIAGRAM A

DIAGRAM B

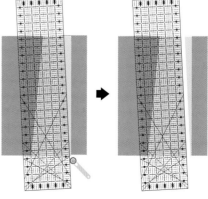

DIAGRAM C

DIAGRAM D

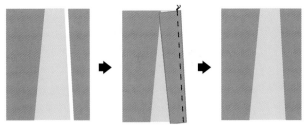

DIAGRAM E

DIAGRAM F

COMPLETED TOP

you want the angle of the cut to be, which will tell you how much to overlap the fabrics before cutting.

At the end of this step, you should have a pieced strip measuring 58″ long.

6. Assemble two more 58″ strips in the same manner, loosely basing your piecing on **Diagram F** but using your own variations in widths and angles. Using the same fabric for the first and last pieces in each strip is a nice way to unify the design.

ASSEMBLING THE QUILT TOP

7. Decide how you'd like your three strips arranged. Having the angles at the top and bottom of each strip alternate as shown in **Completed Top** helps unify the design. Sew the strips together and press the seam allowances to one side or open.

BACKING AND FINISHING

Make a 50″ × 62″ backing. Build a quilt sandwich and quilt. Cut six 2″ strips from your binding fabric and bind your quilt. (Refer to the Finishing Your Quilt section on page 159 as needed.)

Ideas for Quilting

- A hand-quilted chunky running stitch would be fun, running along each of the angles of one fabric.
- Improvisational piecing calls for improvisational quilting! Try quilting random lines and circles.
- As a simple and dramatic option, you could stitch horizontal lines across the quilt in varying widths. This treatment would add a lot of texture to the design as well.

Creative Exercise:
FINDING YOUR PERSONAL QUILTING STYLE

When you describe your style as a quilter, you can certainly use the descriptors we all tend to use: *modern, traditional, minimalist, primitive,* and so on. But here's what's really interesting about your personal quilting style: it goes deeper than those words. Your style contains visual and emotional elements that are woven throughout your entire life.

Here's one way to tease out what those elements are and get a better handle on your style. First, get a stack of old magazines—ideally, ones you don't mind cutting up—that cover a wide variety of subjects. Get some scissors, a good-size piece of poster board, and some glue sticks. Pour your favorite beverage and put on some music you love. Then, relax, sip, and slowly flip through those magazines. Every time you hit upon an image, color, word, graphic, or anything else that jumps out at you, tear it out and set it aside. Don't think about this too much; just act on your impulses. By the time you've been through all the magazines, you'll have a nice little pile of images, and these are the seeds of your unique vision. (You might also need another beverage.)

Now, set the poster board in front of you and start arranging the images on it. Play around with them, moving them about, cutting bits off, combining them with other images. Once again, don't overthink this process. Remember, you aren't making fine art here; you're making a collage that pleases you. Everything you paste down should make you feel happy.

When your collage is done, step back and view it from a little distance. Grab your quilt journal and write down the answers to these questions: What colors are prominent in this collage? Are there any visual symbols (flowers, cats, houses, etc.) that show up again and again? How would you describe the mood of this collage? Do you see intricacy or simplicity? Large-scale objects or small-scale ones? Straight lines or curving ones? Do you see boldness or subtlety, or something in between?

. . . And, given all that information, how would you describe your quilting style now?

How Do You Describe Your Quilting Style?

"I'd say that my style is modern for sure. I love bold geometric designs that make a big impact. The bigger the better. Mixing linen with my cotton prints helps add a modern touch to my quilt designs. The contrast of the simple clean look of linen with a mix of bold, happy prints really defines my style."

Rashida Coleman-Hale,
iheartlinen.typepad.com

"My style of quilting is more traditional, with a touch of whimsy thrown in. I love to incorporate appliqué into my quilting as often as possible, which is where the whimsical element comes in, though it does add to the amount of time invested in a project. I like to try new and different techniques and I shy away from anything that looks too contemporary or modern."

Julie Cefalu, thecraftyquilter.com

"I like using simple, modern clean lines, and bright colors mixed with quieter ones so everything can breathe a little bit. Whether I'm quilting improvisationally or using a favorite pattern like log cabin or string piecing, I love it when my fabrics tell me what to do next. I've been so fortunate to study with Denyse Schmidt several times now, and drawing on that creative improvisational process and energy has really fueled my work. And although I admire intricate piecing and quilting so much in others' work, I feel like I can't fight fate—my simple style just works for me."

Susan Beal, westcoastcrafty.com

"My quilting style runs the spectrum from elaborate, embellished quilted art to projects that are very quick and simple. As a classically trained visual artist, I especially enjoy working with complex design elements in my art quilts, and I love to include unusual and surprising details that 'reward' a viewer who takes a closer look at my work."

Meryl Ann Butler, merylannbutler.com

"Most of the quilts I'm drawn to have that more traditional style of blocks and setting. Although I like to mix it up a little bit with bright and modern fabrics, or omitting sashing and so on, I don't feel as comfortable with the slicker, or improvisational, look of true modern quilts. Give me an old-fashioned block book and I'm in my element!"

Katy Jones, fatquarterly.com,
imagingermonkey.blogspot.co.uk

"My easygoing, modern-meets-traditional quilting style is a lot like my lifestyle—feet are welcome on the coffee table, as long as they're bare feet. My quilting style is also a reflection of how I live, with dashes of happiness, splashes of absurdity, and heaps of merriment."

Monica Solorio-Snow, thehappyzombie.com

The PATCHWORK DIAMONDS QUILT

FINISHED BLOCK SIZE: THIS QUILT IS ASSEMBLED IN ROWS
RATHER THAN BLOCKS.
FINISHED QUILT SIZE: 44" X 64"

CHRISTINA: *"Normally, when I design a quilt, I have a pretty precise placement in mind for the various fabrics. But with this quilt, I suggest tossing all the print squares into a paper bag and then drawing them out one at a time, letting randomness play a part in the design. (Although you could definitely move things around if the same fabric shows up too much in one row. No need to be strict about it!)"*

DIANE: *"I find it so easy to become obsessed with how this fabric looks next to that one, I rather like the idea of handing most of the control over to the paper bag!"*

Skill Level:

PIECED BY LIZ HUTTON

SUPPLIES

Background: 2½ yards white solid
Diamonds: 8 fat quarters various prints
Backing: 2¾ yards your choice of fabric
Binding: ½ yard your choice of fabric
Batting: 48" × 68" (twin size)

FABRICS USED HERE

Windham Fabrics: Floursack
FreeSpirit Fabrics: Designer Solids Arctic White

CUTTING THE FABRICS

Background/White Solid:
See page 154 for more on cutting sashing and border strips. Cutting from the selvage edge, cut 16 strips, 2" × the length of your fabric. Then, subcut them into these units:
Cut 3 strips down to 2" × 62".
Cut 2 strips down to 4 lengths, 2 measuring 2" × 51" and 2 measuring 2" × 6".
Cut 2 strips down to 4 lengths, 2 measuring 2" × 42" and 2 measuring 2" × 15".
Cut 2 strips down to 4 lengths, 2 measuring 2" × 33" and 2 measuring 2" × 24".
Cut 7 strips down to 123 pieces, each measuring 2" × 3½".

Prints (cut all pieces below from each print):
Cut 5 strips, 3½" × 22".
Subcut them to 30 squares, each measuring 3½" × 3½". Repeat this process for all prints.
Cut 15 of these print squares in half on the diagonal, creating 30 half square triangles.

ASSEMBLING THE QUILT ROWS

1. Use **Diagram A** throughout this step. Begin the first row by sewing a print triangle to a 3½" background strip. Next, sew on a print square, another background strip, and another print triangle to the row. Press all seam allowances toward the prints.

Sew a 2" × 6" sashing strip to the top (6") edge of this unit, pressing the seam allowance toward the unit. Next, center a print square on top of the 6" strip and sew them together. Press the seam allowance toward the print square.

Place a ruler over this finished unit, lining it up with the angle of one of the print triangles. Cut through the solid strip and the print square at the same angle. Repeat this process to trim the other side. This step creates the top right corner of your quilt top, or Row 1. Repeat this process to create the bottom left corner of your quilt top, or Row 15.

2. Sew two print triangles and three print squares together, placing 3½" background strips between them. Press the seam allowances toward the prints. Make sure both triangles are oriented as shown in **Diagram B**.

Sew a 2" × 15" sashing strip to the top (15") edge of the row and press the seam allowance toward the prints. Trim the sashing strip along the angle of the print triangles as you did for Row 1. Repeat this step to create a second row—these will be Rows 2 and 14.

3. Repeat the process in Step 2 to continue assembling rows, using **Diagram C** for placement and the block counts listed below. Pay attention to print triangle orientation, especially for Rows 7, 8, and 9. Press all seam allowances toward the prints and cut the sashing strips to match the angles of the triangles on each end. Here are the numbers of pieces you'll need for each row:

- Row 3 and Row 13: 2 print tri-

Ideas for Quilting

- Try an allover stippled pattern.
- You could add a contrast to the straight lines of this quilt by stitching a decorative pattern, such as leaves on a vine.
- For a simpler option, try quilting in straight lines ¼" outside the edges of all the sashing strips running both directions, and through the print squares.

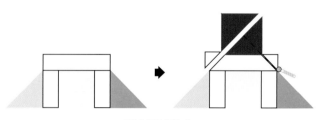

DIAGRAM A

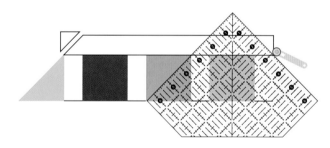

DIAGRAM B

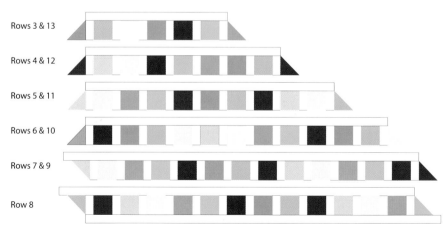

Rows 3 & 13

Rows 4 & 12

Rows 5 & 11

Rows 6 & 10

Rows 7 & 9

Row 8

DIAGRAM C

angles, 5 print squares, and 6 small background strips; one 2″ × 24″ sashing strip.

- Row 4 and Row 12: 2 print triangles, 7 print squares, and 8 small background strips; one 2″ × 33″ sashing strip.
- Row 5 and Row 11: 2 print triangles, 9 print squares, and 10 small background strips; one 2″ × 42″ sashing strip.
- Row 6 and Row 10: 2 print triangles, 11 print squares, and 12 small background strips; one 2″ × 51″ sashing strip.

Rows 7, 8, and 9 have important differences in how the sashing strips are sewn. In Row 8 you'll be sewing a sashing strip to the top and bottom of the print strip. In Rows 7, 8, and 9 the sashing strips extend beyond the end of the print strip on one side, for extra fabric to cut angles. When you sew these strips, begin stitching at the flush end and finish at the excess strip.

- Row 7 and Row 9: 2 print triangles, 12 print squares, and 13 small background strips; one 2″ × 62″ sashing strip.

- Row 8: 2 print triangles, 12 print squares, and 13 small background strips; two 2″ × 62″ sashing strips.

ASSEMBLING THE QUILT TOP

4. To begin, sew Rows 1 and 2 together **(Diagram D)**. Add Rows 3 through 8 one at a time to form the first section. Press all seam allowances toward the print strips.

5. Next, repeat the process in Step 4 to sew Rows 9 through 15 together into a separate section. Sew the two sections together to complete the quilt top. Press the seam allowance toward the print strip.

BACKING AND FINISHING

Make a 48″ × 68″ backing. Build a quilt sandwich and quilt. Cut six 2″ strips from your binding fabric and bind your quilt. (Refer to the Finishing Your Quilt section on page 159 as needed.)

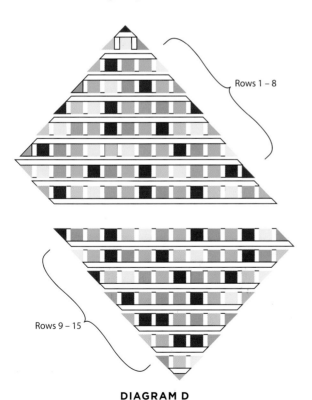

Rows 1 – 8

Rows 9 – 15

DIAGRAM D

COMPLETED TOP

QUIZ

Get to Know Your Inner Quilter

Creative processes like quilt design or fabric selection so often run on emotional responses, hunches, and instincts—and this is hard stuff to put into words sometimes. This handy quiz should give you some new insights to mull over.

1. Imagine you're at the fabric store with an unlimited budget. (Hmm, maybe we'll join you in that scenario!) What do the fabric bolts stacked up in your shopping cart look like?

a. Lots of stripes and checks, crisp solids and plenty of neutrals.

b. It's a mixed bag! I'm grabbing everything that appeals to my eye in the moment.

c. They're all drenched in bold colors, because I don't do neutrals.

d. There are way more prints than solids.

2. Let's take a look at your quilting tools now. Which of the following best describes them?

a. I have a place for everything, and everything's in its place. Woe unto anyone who misplaces one of my tools!

b. They're around here somewhere.

c. I always get the pins with the prettiest heads, and I picked out my rotary cutter because its handle color coordinated so nicely with the handle of my fabric scissors.

d. I bought a toolbox with separate compartments to store things in just because everything looks so nice laid out in rows.

3. When you look at a handmade quilt, what's the very first thing that jumps out at you? (Don't overthink this, now; first impressions are best.)

a. I look at the workmanship. How well do all the seams match up? Is the binding nice and even?

b. I don't really look at any specific details; I just take in the overall artistic impression of the thing.

c. I look at all the colors! I'll walk across a room to check out a colorful quilt.

d. I immediately start scrutinizing how the blocks are put together.

4. Switching gears a little, then: If you were to plant a garden, what would it look like?

a. I'd have neat rows of plants, organized by their type and height so that no plant would cast too much shade on any others.

b. I'd plant one of every kind of plant that appealed to me at the plant store. If some of them died, I'd just plant something else. I hope I'd remember to water it!

c. I'd plant the biggest, showiest flowers I could find, and lots of them. I'd mix the colors all together like a big, flowery mosaic.

d. I'd plant one of those Renaissance knot gardens, where there are low hedges grown in a flowerlike pattern, with different plants filling up each section.

Here's how to add up your score: Give yourself 5 points for each "a" answer, 10 points for each "b" answer, 15 points for each "c," and 20 points for each "d." Match your total score up with the numbers below.

20–38 Points: If this is your score, you tend to be precision oriented in quilting. You like to measure twice (or three times) before you cut. You like your seams to match up perfectly, and you don't mind ripping out and doing over. You'd find some fun challenges in the Can't Help Myself Quilt on page 35 and the Zig Zag Zig Quilt on page 62.

39–53 Points: You're a pretty loose and serendipitous quilter. You're also not a huge fan of measuring things, and sometimes you have "happy accidents" while quilting. There's nothing in the world wrong with having a more casual quilting style. In fact, sometimes letting go of the rules is a gateway to exciting creative places! See what happens when you undertake the Crazy Strips Quilt on page 42 or the Squared In Quilt on page 112.

54–67 Points: Clearly, you're attracted to color! Your score reveals that you gravitate to fabrics with rich hues and quilt designs that let you play with the effects of this color next to that one. You'd enjoy creating the Bric-a-Brac Quilt (page 73) or the Cross-Stitch Quilt (page 28).

68–80 Points: If this is your score, your mind's eye sees patterns all around you. You love shapes and how they fit together to create intriguing visual environments. You'd have fun piecing the Odds and Ends Quilt (page 137) or the Elevator Music Quilt (page 13).

The POCKET WALL CADDY

FINISHED PROJECT SIZE: 7½" X 23"

CHRISTINA: *"This project is based on a wall caddy my grandmother keeps on her sewing room wall. It's been there for as long as I can remember, and when I see this version on my studio wall now, it's a nice reminder of her."*

DIANE: *"I have some cotton scraps that belonged to my great grandmother—they'd make such a nice basis for a wall caddy like this!"*

Skill Level:

SUPPLIES

Background: ¼ yard lightweight canvas

Pockets: 5 fat quarters or large scraps coordinating prints

Backing: ¼ yard coordinating print

Binding: ¼ yard coordinating print

Interfacing: ½ yard Pellon Fusible Featherweight

Batting: leftover scraps, see dimensions in Cutting the Fabrics

Dowel: ¼" to ½" diameter, two 9" lengths

Ribbon: ¼" wide, 12" length

FABRICS USED HERE

Kokka Fabrics: Canvas (light upholstery weight)

Kokka Fabrics: Trefle Blue Stripes

Lecien: Gingham Birds

Art Gallery Fabrics: Summerlove Sweet Days Mist by Pat Bravo

Moda: Sunkissed Sweetwater Dots

Blue Hill Fabrics: Savannah c.1890 by Sarah Morgan

CUTTING THE FABRICS

Background:

Cut 1 canvas piece, 7½" × 27".

Cut 1 batting piece, 7½" × 27".

Cut 1 backing piece, 7½" × 27".

Pocket A:

Cut 1 print piece, 4" × 7½".

Cut 1 batting piece, 3½" × 3½".

Pocket B (Star):

From star background print, cut the following: 2 squares, each measuring 4" × 4"; 4 squares, each measuring 2¼" × 2¼"; 1 square measuring 7½" × 7½".

From the star print, cut 3 squares, each measuring 4" × 4".

Cut 1 batting piece, 7" × 7".

Pocket C:

Cut 1 print piece, 8½" × 7½".

Cut 1 batting piece, 3⅞" × 7".

Pocket D:

Cut 1 print piece, 6½" × 7½".

Cut 1 batting piece, 2⅞" × 7".

Finishing:

Interfacing: Cut 2 pieces, each measuring 7½" × 20".

Binding: Cut 2 strips, each measuring 1½" × 28".

ASSEMBLING THE WALL CADDY POCKETS
POCKET A

This pocket will adorn the larger star pocket at the top of the caddy.

1. Use **Diagram A** for Steps 1 and 2. Fold the 4" × 7½" Pocket A piece in half with *wrong* sides facing. Slip the 3½" × 3½" piece of batting into the folded fabric, making sure it's snug in the fold and ¼" from each edge of the fabric. Press the fold with a hot steam iron. The piece now measures 4" × 3¾".

2. Edge stitch across the top edge of the pocket, ¼" from the fold. Stitch an "X" across the pocket, starting at the stitching you just did and going down to the corners.

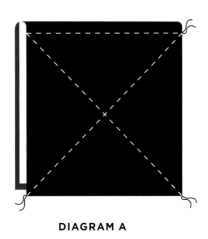

DIAGRAM A

POCKET B (STAR POCKET)

We'll refer to Half Square Triangles as HSTs. For details on how to assemble them, see page 155.

3. Pair up one 4" × 4" star background print with one 4" × 4" star print and assemble them into four HSTs. Repeat this process to make another four HSTs, for eight total. Square each HST to 2¼" × 2¼". Press half the seam allowances toward the star background print and half toward the star print. (This will help you match them up in the next step.)

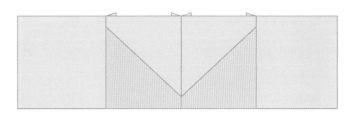

DIAGRAM B

4. Use **Diagram B** for Steps 4 and 5. Pair up two HSTs that have their seam allowances pressed in opposite directions. Sew them together, taking care to nestle the seams (see page 157). Press the seam allowance open. Repeat this process with the rest of the HSTs to create four pairs.

Christina's Tips

- Use a walking foot on your sewing machine for sewing fabric and batting together with no backing. The walking foot is also handy for adding binding.
- You might want to try using Dritz Wonder Tape, which is a double-sided adhesive that makes binding easier. Once you've sewn the binding to the front side of your caddy, put a strip of Wonder Tape on the back side, just inside the stitching line. Press the binding onto the Wonder Tape to cover and stick it down. Then, stitch in the ditch on the front side next to the binding, making sure your stitching is catching the binding on the back.
- You'll need an erasable marking tool for this project. We recommend a FriXion pen, which erases with the heat of your iron.
- To give this project an especially nice finish, look for "dowel finials" or "dowel caps," which are wooden shapes you can glue to the ends of your dowels. (See the Resources section on page 169.)

5. Sew a 2¼" background square to each end of two HST pairs. Press the seam allowances toward the HSTs. These two units will form the sides of your star block.

6. Use **Diagram C** for Steps 6 through 8. Sew another HST pair to the top of the 4" × 4" star print square. Press the seam allowance toward the HST unit.

7. Now, place this unit right side up on your work surface. Place Pocket A on top of the 4" × 4" star print square, matching and pinning the side and bottom edges. Pin another HST unit to the bottom edge of the pocket with right sides facing. Sew along the bottom edge and press the seam allowance toward the HST unit.

8. Sew the side units from Step 5 to the left and right edges, being sure to capture the sides of the pocket in the seam allowance. Press the seam allowances toward the side units. Trim the batting out of the seam allowances to reduce bulk. Your finished star block should measure 7½" × 7½".

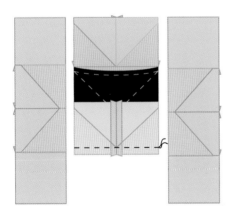

DIAGRAM C

9. Place the star block on your ironing board, wrong side up. Center the 7" × 7" piece of batting over the star (the batting should be at least ¼" from each edge). Turn these pieces over together and press them with a hot steam iron. Place a few pins to hold the two layers together, and quilt the star.

10. Pin the 7½" × 7½" background square to the finished star block, right sides facing. Make sure Pocket A opens toward the top! Sew through all layers along the top and bottom edges. Then, turn the piece right side out and press the top and bottom seams flat.

11. Stitch along the top of the star pocket, ¼" from the edge.

POCKET C

Use **Diagram D** for Pockets C and D.

12. Fold the 8½" × 7½" Pocket C print in half crosswise with right sides facing. Sew along the long edge, so the piece now measures 4¼" × 7½". Press the seam open and then turn the piece right side out. Press it flat, centering the seam along one side.

Slip the 3⅞" × 7" piece of batting into this fabric sleeve, so it's snug in the folds and ¼" from each side. Press this fabric/batting sandwich with a hot steam iron and then edge stitch ¼" from the top.

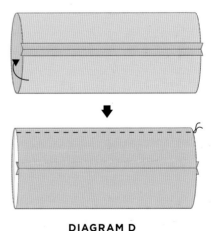

DIAGRAM D

POCKET D

13. Fold the 6½" × 7½" Pocket D print in half crosswise with right sides facing. Sew along the long edge, so the piece measures 3¼" × 7½". Press the seam allowance open and turn the piece right side out. Press it flat, centering the seam along one side. Slip the $2^7/8'' \times 7''$ piece of batting into the fabric sleeve, so it's snug in the folds and $1/4''$ from each side. Press this fabric/batting sandwich with a hot steam iron and then edge stitch $1/4''$ from the top.

ASSEMBLING THE WALL CADDY

Use **Diagram E** for Steps 14 through 17.

14. Fuse a piece of interfacing to the back side of the canvas piece, lining it up with the top, right, and left edges of the canvas. (Follow the manufacturer's directions for fusing.) Trim the second piece of interfacing so it covers the remainder of the canvas, and fuse.

15. Lay the $7^1/2'' \times 27''$ piece of batting on your ironing board, then center the canvas over it, right side up. Press them together with a hot steam iron. Trim away any excess batting and place a pin at the top, bottom, and center to hold the layers in place.

16. Position the star pocket (Pocket B) on the canvas piece, making sure it opens toward the top. Pocket B's top edge should be $2^3/4''$ from the top edge of the canvas. Match and pin the raw side edges. Stitch across the bottom of the pocket through all the layers, a scant $1/16''$ from the edge. Don't remove the side pins yet.

17. Place Pocket C on the canvas, with its top edge $2^3/4''$ below the bottom edge of Pocket B. Match and pin the raw side edges, and then stitch across the bottom of the pocket through all layers a scant $1/16''$ from the edge. Lay a ruler over Pocket C and measure $1^3/4''$ in from its left edge. Draw a vertical line at this point with an erasable marking tool. Measure $1^1/2''$ in from that line and draw another line. Stitch through all layers along both of these lines. Keep the side pins in place for now.

To get a nice finish with this stitching, leave a few inches of thread tail at the start of your seam. Start the seam with your needle in the canvas

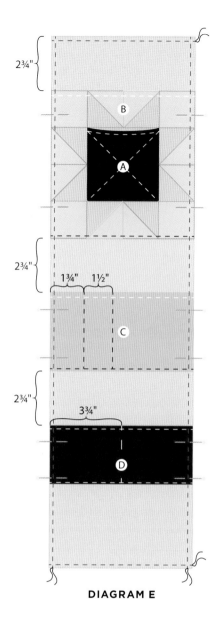

DIAGRAM E

right at the top of the pocket. Stitch forward one stitch, then backstitch one stitch. Continue stitching forward until you reach the bottom edge of the pocket. Backstitch one stitch and then forward stitch one stitch; then clip your thread, leaving another long tail. Don't trim these thread tails yet; you'll do it after sewing on the next pocket.

18. Place Pocket D on the canvas, positioning its top edge $2^3/4''$ below the bottom edge of Pocket C. Match and pin the side edges, and then stitch across the bottom of the pocket through all layers a scant $1/16''$ from the edge. Lay a ruler over Pocket

C and measure 3¾" in from its left edge. Draw a line at this point with an erasable marking tool and then stitch along this line in the same manner as in Step 17. Baste through all layers along both sides, starting at the bottom and sewing to the top. Remove all side pins.

19. Flip the piece over so the back is facing up. Gently pull the back thread tails from the pocket stitching. As you pull, a small loop of thread will appear. Use the tip of your seam ripper to grab it and pull it through to the back. Knot each pair of thread tails twice and then trim them so a little bit of thread extends beyond the knots. Flip the piece back over now and press it to set the stitches.

20. Layer the assembled canvas with the 7½" × 27" backing print, *wrong* sides together, matching and pinning all four edges. Baste along the top and bottom edges through all layers.

21. Bind the sides of the caddy. Sew a binding strip to the right and left edges using a ¼" seam allowance **(Diagram F)**. Press the binding away from the caddy, and then fold the raw edge of the binding so it just meets the raw edge of the caddy. Press this fold and then repeat this process on the opposite side. Now, fold the binding strip to the

back of the caddy and secure it with a blind stitch (see page 167).

FINISHING THE WALL CADDY

22. Trim the excess binding from the top and bottom of the caddy. Place it on your ironing board with the back side facing up. Fold the top of the caddy down ½" and press the fold. Measure down 1" from this folded edge and fold the top down again to this line. Press the fold and pin it in place. Stitch through all layers a scant ¹⁄₁₆" from the bottom fold of this sleeve. Repeat this process to create another sleeve at the bottom of the caddy. Be careful that you don't stitch through the bottom of Pocket D when you sew the sleeve.

23. Insert a 9" dowel into each sleeve, and tie the ends of the ribbon around the top dowel to form a loop for hanging.

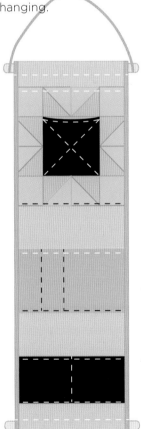

COMPLETED WALL CADDY

DIAGRAM F

MAKING QUILTS WORK FOR YOU

Sometimes you see a quilt design you really love, but your skills aren't quite up to it yet. That doesn't mean you can't make it! There are lots of simple ways to modify a pattern so it fits your quilting style right now. And many of these techniques can also help you put your own stylistic stamp on a quilt.

- If you're feeling intimidated by a complex pattern, why not make just half of it—or even a quarter, or just one block? That section can become a lovely baby quilt, lap quilt, or table decoration (not to mention tote bag, wall art, or pillow), and you get to try your hand at a new level of quilting.

- If the notion of coming up with a color scheme for a quilt intimidates you, just reduce the number of colors you use. All of the designs in this book would be interesting pieced in just two or three colors. Or, you can always use a solid background and one print and end up with a very beautiful quilt.

- If a quilt involves curved seams but you aren't quite proficient at them yet, just cut the curved shapes from fabric and use some fusible webbing to fuse them to a base block. You'll get the same effect with much less work.

- If you aren't comfortable with free-motion quilting in intricate patterns, try tie quilting instead. You can arrange the ties in all kinds of interesting designs, and you won't even need a sewing machine. If you don't like the look of tied yarn, how about making simple cross stitches with embroidery floss? (See page 163 for more on tie quilting.)

- If you're not a big fan of measuring things or being precise, why not try making any of the designs in this book in a "wonky" style? If you deliberately make edges crooked and points not match up, you can end up with a whole new design—one that looks fun and casual.

Every new quilt begins with excitement, high hopes, and neatly folded stacks of beautiful fabric. It's always fun to dream of the moment when you'll snuggle beneath the finished quilt and admire your lovely piecing.

But some projects, as many of us have experienced, take a hard left turn somewhere along the way. Those fabrics that worked so well together as yardage suddenly seem to be fighting with each other as patchwork. The design you adored for the first three blocks suddenly feels stale by the sixth. You become utterly sick of trying to match up those darn points.

It's no fun when this happens, and we often compound that by feeling guilty. What about our investment in supplies? What about the time we've wasted? What does it say about us as creative people, that we can't even finish a project? Before long, this poor, troubled project becomes fraught with emotion.

This is a great moment to give that quilt a long nap. Put it away, preferably someplace you can't see it. You need time for your feelings about failing and not finishing to dissolve, and this could take months or even years. And

please, don't feel one bit of guilt over having an unfinished project sitting around! Some creative processes simply need more simmering time than others. When you can think of this work-in-progress without the pangs of guilt or frustration, then it's time to pull it back out.

Sometimes, that's all it takes to revive a project—you'll spread out the pieces you had finished, and suddenly be able to see lots of possibilities. Maybe you're ready to tackle that piecing again. Maybe changing the color of the sashing pulls all those colors in the blocks together. Maybe you'd rather take the blocks you've finished and make them into a smaller project.

Or maybe, after that long respite, you'll realize that you truly don't want to proceed with this quilt. This is fine, too! Some creative processes exist only to teach us a valuable lesson in design or technique—a lesson we'll use in future quilts. Maybe you can donate this unfinished project to a local charity quilting group, so it finds a good home. Then, take a deep breath and, your lessons learned, move forward in your quilting adventures.

The ZIG ZAG ZIG QUILT

FINISHED BLOCK SIZE: THIS QUILT IS ASSEMBLED IN ROWS
RATHER THAN BLOCKS.
FINISHED QUILT SIZE: 42" X 54"

DIANE: *"Wow, you can really get lost in all the wonderful shapes created by these zigzags."*

CHRISTINA: *"Yes, and it's a very meditative kind of quilt to make. This is one of those projects where you'll need to take your time, stay present, and rejoice at each successful point, diamond, and zigzag that appears."*

DIANE: *"There's something very soothing in that kind of deep focus. I like a project that makes you slow down and truly experience the quilting process."*

Skill Level:

SUPPLIES

Cream Solid: 1 yard
Aqua Solid: ½ yard
Green Solid: 1 yard
Blue Solid: ¾ yard
Navy Solid: ¾ yard
Gray Solid: ¾ yard
Backing: 2¾ yards your choice of
    fabric
Binding: ½ yard your choice of
    fabric
Batting: 46" × 60" (crib/baby size)
Templates A, B, and C (located on
    page 171)

FABRICS USED HERE

Robert Kaufman Kona Cotton: Bone,
    Charcoal, Teal Blue
FreeSpirit Designer Solids: Aqua,
    Caribbean Sea, Chartreuse

CUTTING THE FABRICS

Cream Solid:
Cut 3 strips, 5¼" × width of fabric.
    Cut 34 Template A pieces from
    them.
Cut 4 strips, 3" × width of fabric.
    Cut 32 Template B pieces and 18
    Template C pieces from them.

Aqua Solid:
Cut 1 strip, 5¼" × width of fabric.
    Cut 9 Template A pieces.

Green Solid:
Cut 3 strips, 5¼" × width of fabric.
    Cut 25 Template A pieces from
    them.
Cut 4 strips, 3" × width of fabric.
    Cut 24 Template B pieces and 18
    Template C pieces from them.

Blue Solid:
Cut 3 strips, 5¼" × width of fabric.
    Cut 26 Template A pieces from
    them.
Cut 2 strips, 3" × width of fabric.
    Cut 32 Template B pieces from
    them.

Navy Solid:
Cut 2 strips, 5¼" × width of fabric.
    Cut 16 Template A pieces from
    them.
Cut 3 strips, 3" × width of fabric.
    Cut 16 Template B pieces and 18
    Template C pieces from them.

Gray Solid:
Cut 3 strips, 5¼" × width of fabric.
    Cut 26 Template A pieces from
    them.
Cut 3 strips, 3" × width of fabric.
    Cut 16 Template B pieces and 18
    Template C pieces from them.

Christina's Tips

- For this quilt top, you'll want to make especially sure your sewing machine is producing accurate ¼" seams (see page 154).

- You'll see the term "dog ear" in these instructions. A dog ear is the bit of seam allowance from the angle pieces that extends above your piecing after you press the seam allowance (see the diagram). Normally you might trim these off, but with this quilt, the dog ears give you helpful points of alignment.

DOG EAR

- Before sewing the rows of your quilt together, check that you have ¼" of fabric above the points where the seams meet, as shown in the diagram. This way, when you sew the rows together, the points will meet up with the seam perfectly.

¼" SEAM ALLOWANCE

- If you look at the backs of your pieced rows, you'll be able to see an "X" where the seams of your points meet, as shown in the diagram. These are key points: When you're sewing the rows together, make sure your stitching goes through each "X" along the row.

APEX X

ASSEMBLING THE QUILT ROWS

This design is composed of four row designs and four sections. Each row design is repeated in each section, but with a different fabric arrangement. As you complete each row, label it with its section and row number, so it's easier to assemble the quilt later on.

SECTION 1, ROW 1

Use Template A (triangle) pieces in aqua, cream, and green. Use **Diagram A**.

1. Sew a cream triangle to an aqua triangle, matching the edges. Press the seam allowance toward the aqua triangle. Place an aqua triangle on top of the cream triangle. Here's where that "dog ear" comes into play: When you match the edges of the triangles, align the top point of the aqua triangle with the dog ear from your last seam. Sew and press the seam allowance toward the aqua triangle.

2. Stop and make sure the top edges of your piecing are forming a straight line—do this little check with each new piece you add.

3. Next, add one green and one aqua triangle. Press the seam allowances toward the aqua triangles.

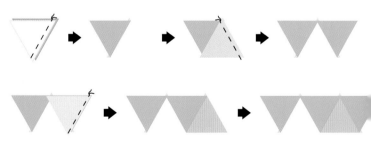

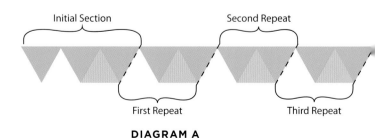

DIAGRAM A

Repeat this process three more times, starting with a cream triangle and following the color order in **Diagram A**, until you have four cream, four green, and nine aqua triangles in the row.

Use Template B (triangle) pieces in cream, gray, and aqua, and Template C (diamond) pieces in green. Use **Diagram B**.

4. Place a green diamond on your work surface right side up, with the points to the top left and bottom right. Place a cream triangle on top of the diamond, matching the right and bottom edges. Sew and press the seam allowance toward the green diamond.

5. Stop and make sure the top edges of these pieces form a straight line. If they don't, take them apart and try again.

6. Now, place a gray triangle on top of the cream triangle, matching the right and top edges. Sew them together and press the seam allowance toward the gray triangle. Sew a cream triangle to the gray triangle, pressing the seam allowance toward the gray triangle. Place a green diamond on top of the cream triangle, matching up the bottom point of the green diamond with the dog ear at the bottom point of the cream triangle. Notice that the right edge of the green diamond will fall short of reaching the top right point of the cream triangle by 1/4", as shown in the inset in **Diagram B**. Sew them together and press the seam allowance toward the green diamond.

7. Sew an aqua triangle to the green diamond. Press the seam allowance toward the green diamond. Place a green diamond on the aqua triangle, matching the top point of the green diamond with the dog ear at the top of the aqua triangle. The

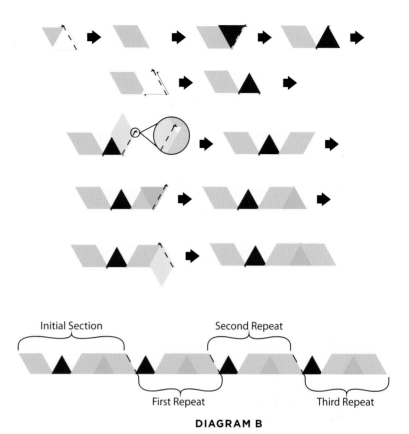

DIAGRAM B

right edge will again fall short of the bottom right point of the aqua triangle. Sew and press the seam allowance toward the green diamond. Repeat this process three more times, starting with a cream triangle and following the color order in **Diagram B**, until you have four gray triangles, four aqua triangles, eight cream triangles, and nine green diamonds in the row.

SECTION 1, ROW 3
Use Template B (triangle) pieces in cream, gray, and aqua, and Template C (diamond) pieces in green. Use **Diagram C** for placement, and refer back to Diagram B for piecing details.

8. Orient a green diamond with the points to the top left and bottom right. Sew a gray triangle to the green diamond and press the seam allowance toward the green diamond. Add another green diamond, pressing the seam allowance toward the green diamond.

9. Add a cream triangle, an aqua triangle, a cream triangle, and a green diamond. Press the seam allowances toward the aqua triangles and green diamond.

10. Repeat this process three more times, starting with a gray triangle and following the color order in **Diagram C**, until you have four gray triangles, four aqua triangles, eight cream triangles, and nine green diamonds in the row.

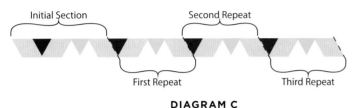

DIAGRAM C

SECTION 1, ROW 4

Use Template A (triangle) pieces in gray, green, and cream. Use **Diagram D** for placement and refer back to Diagram A for piecing details.

11. Sew a green triangle to a gray triangle, pressing the seam allowance toward the green triangle. Add a gray triangle, a cream triangle, and a gray triangle, pressing the seam allowances toward the green and cream triangles.

Repeat this process three more times, starting with a green triangle and following the color order in **Diagram D**, until you have four green, four cream, and nine gray triangles in the row.

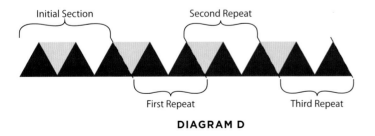

DIAGRAM D

SECTION 2, ROW 1

Use Template A (triangle) pieces in gray, navy, and blue. Use **Diagram E**.

12. Sew a navy triangle to a gray triangle, pressing the seam allowance toward the gray triangle. Add a gray triangle, a blue triangle, and a gray triangle, pressing the seam allowances toward the gray triangles.

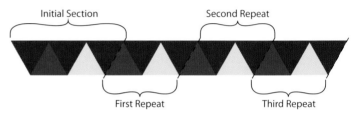

DIAGRAM E

13. Repeat this process three more times, starting with a navy triangle and following the color order in **Diagram E**, until you have four navy, four blue, and nine gray triangles in the row.

SECTION 2, ROW 2

Use Template B (triangle) pieces in gray, blue, and cream, and Template C (diamond) pieces in navy. Use **Diagram F** for placement, and refer back to Diagram B for piecing details.

14. Orient a navy diamond with the points to the bottom left and top right. Sew a gray triangle to the navy diamond and press the seam allowance toward the gray triangle. Add a navy diamond, blue triangle, cream triangle, blue triangle, and navy diamond, pressing the seam allowances toward the gray and blue triangles.

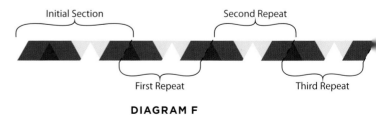

DIAGRAM F

15. Repeat this process three more times, starting with a gray triangle and following the color order in **Diagram F**, until you have four gray triangles, four cream triangles, eight blue triangles, and nine navy diamonds in the row.

SECTION 2, ROW 3

Use Template B (triangle) pieces in blue, gray, and cream, and Template C (diamond) pieces in navy. Use **Diagram G**.

16. Orient a navy diamond with the points to the bottom left and top right. Sew a blue triangle to the navy diamond, pressing the seam allowance toward the blue triangle. Add a gray triangle, a blue triangle, a navy diamond, and a cream triangle, pressing the seam allowances toward the blue and cream triangles.

17. Repeat this process three more times, starting with a navy diamond and following the color order in **Diagram G**, until you have four gray triangles, four cream triangles, eight blue triangles, and nine navy diamonds in the row.

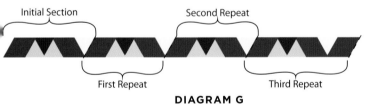

DIAGRAM G

SECTION 2, ROW 4

Use Template A (triangle) pieces in cream, blue, and navy. Use **Diagram H**.

18. Sew together a cream triangle, blue triangle, cream triangle, navy triangle, and cream triangle, pressing the seam allowances toward the cream triangles.

19. Repeat this process three more times, starting with a blue triangle and following the color order

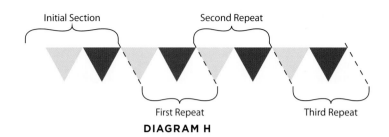

DIAGRAM H

in **Diagram H**, until you have four blue, four navy, and nine cream triangles in the row.

SECTION 3, ROW 1

Use Template A (triangle) pieces in cream, green, and gray. Use **Diagram I**.

20. Sew together a cream triangle, green triangle, cream triangle, gray triangle, and cream triangle. Press the seam allowances toward the gray and green triangles.

21. Repeat this process three more times, starting with a green triangle and following the color order in **Diagram I**, until you have four gray, four green, and nine cream triangles in the row.

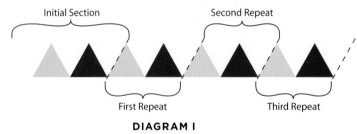

DIAGRAM I

SECTION 3, ROW 2

Use Template B (triangle) pieces in green, blue, and cream, and Template C (diamond) pieces in gray. Use **Diagram J**.

22. Orient a gray diamond with the points to the top left and bottom right. Sew on a green triangle, blue triangle, green triangle, gray diamond, cream triangle, and gray diamond. Press the seam allowances toward the gray diamonds and blue triangles.

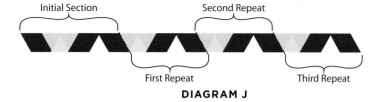

DIAGRAM J

23. Repeat this process three more times, starting with a green triangle and following the color order in **Diagram J**, until you have four blue triangles, four cream triangles, eight green triangles, and nine gray diamonds in the row.

SECTION 3, ROW 3

Use Template B (triangle) pieces in blue, green, and cream, and Template C (diamond) pieces in gray. Use **Diagram K**.

24. Orient a gray diamond with the points to the top left and bottom right. Sew on a blue triangle, gray diamond, green triangle, cream triangle, green triangle, and gray diamond. Press the seam allowances toward the gray diamonds and cream triangles.

25. Repeat this process three more times, starting with a blue triangle and following the color order in **Diagram K**, until you have four blue triangles, four cream triangles, eight green triangles, and nine gray diamonds in the row.

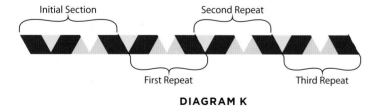

DIAGRAM K

SECTION 3, ROW 4

Use Template A (triangle) pieces in blue, gray, and green. Use **Diagram L**.

26. Sew together a blue triangle, gray triangle, blue triangle, green triangle, and blue triangle. Press the seam allowances toward the gray and green triangles.

27. Repeat this process three more times, starting with a gray triangle and following the color order in **Diagram L**, until you have four gray, four green, and nine blue triangles in the row.

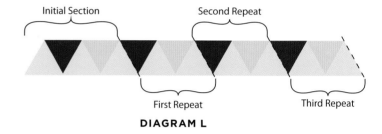

DIAGRAM L

SECTION 4, ROW 1

Use Template A (triangle) pieces in blue, cream, and navy. Use **Diagram M**.

28. Sew together a blue triangle, cream triangle, blue triangle, navy triangle, and blue triangle. Press the seam allowances toward the blue triangles.

29. Repeat this process three more times, starting with a cream triangle and following the color order in **Diagram M**, until you have four cream, four navy, and nine blue triangles in the row.

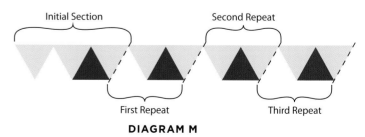

DIAGRAM M

SECTION 4, ROW 2

Use Template B (triangle) pieces in blue, navy, and green, and Template C (diamond) pieces in cream. Use **Diagram N**.

30. Orient a cream diamond with the points to the bottom left and top right. Sew on a blue triangle, cream diamond, navy triangle, green triangle, navy diamond, and cream diamond. Press the seam allowances toward the blue and navy triangles.

31. Repeat this process three more times, starting with a blue triangle and following the color order in **Diagram N**, until you have four blue triangles, four green triangles, eight navy triangles, and nine cream diamonds in the row.

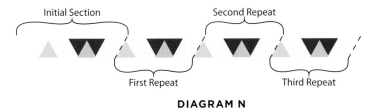

DIAGRAM N

SECTION 4, ROW 3

Use Template B (triangle) pieces in navy, blue, and green, and Template C (diamond) pieces in cream. Use **Diagram O**.

32. Orient a cream diamond with the points to the bottom left and top right. Sew on a navy triangle, blue triangle, navy triangle, cream diamond, green triangle, and cream diamond. Press the seam allowances toward the navy and green triangles.

33. Repeat this process three more times, starting with a navy triangle and following the color order in **Diagram O**, until you have four blue triangles, four green triangles, eight navy triangles, and nine cream diamonds in the row.

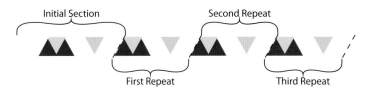

DIAGRAM O

SECTION 4, ROW 4

Use Template A (triangle) pieces in green, navy, and cream. Use **Diagram P**.

34. Sew together a green triangle, navy triangle, green triangle, cream triangle, and green triangle. Press the seam allowances toward the green triangles.

35. Repeat this process three more times, starting with a navy triangle and following the color order in **Diagram P**, until you have four navy, four cream, and nine green triangles in the row.

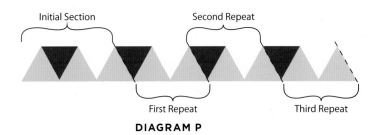

DIAGRAM P

ASSEMBLING THE QUILT TOP

36. Lay out your finished rows, using **Diagram Q** for placement. Begin by assembling the four rows of Section 1.

This is where all that careful pressing you've been doing will pay off. When you sew the rows to each other, you'll be able to nestle the seams easily, because the seam allowances for the same colors will already be pressed in opposite directions. In some cases, the point where the seams match will be about 1/4" in from the raw edge, and in other cases the seams will match right at the raw edge. See page 157 for more on nestling seams. Press the row seam allowances open.

After sewing Rows 1 and 2 together, spread out the piece and double check that all the seams are aligning. If you find some sections are out of alignment, use a seam ripper to remove the row seam in these sections. Gently realign the fabric, nestling and pinning the seams. Sew the section again, backstitching at the beginning and end to secure the seam. Repeat this process to add Row 3 and Row 4 to Section 1.

37. Assemble Sections 2, 3, and 4 in the same manner, being careful to nestle all seams and check their alignment after sewing.

38. Sew Section 1 to Section 2, taking care to nestle all seams. Press the seam allowance open. Sew Section 3 to Section 4 in the same manner. Finally, sew the two quilt top sections together, watching the orientation and seam matching. Press the seam allowance open.

39. If you prefer, you can trim the sides of your finished quilt top at this point, using the dotted lines in **Diagram Q** as a guide. Or, you may prefer to trim the excess fabric when you square your top after quilting.

BACKING AND FINISHING

Make a 46″ × 60″ backing. Build a quilt sandwich and quilt. Cut six 2″ strips from your binding fabric and bind your quilt. (Refer to the Finishing Your Quilt section on page 159 as needed.)

DIAGRAM Q

COMPLETED TOP

Ideas for Quilting

- Straight stitch along the zigzags, ¼" from the seams.
- Quilt vertical lines over the top of the quilt, stretching from top to bottom. Keep them close together for a nice texture.
- Create some contrast by quilting a swirl pattern over the zigzag design.

Tools for Happiness:
PAUSE AND ENJOY

Obviously, most full-size quilts are made over the course of many hours. And although quilting time is generally enjoyable time, it's also easy to become so caught up in the idea of finishing that we work too long, overtax our bodies and minds, and lose the joy in the process.

This may seem like the simplest trick ever, but it really works! Try giving yourself a little schedule of mandatory quilting breaks. Set a timer so it rings once an hour, and when it does, get up, get away from your sewing machine, move your body around, and breathe a little fresh air. Even a ten-minute respite makes a huge difference. Try to think about something other than your quilt-in-progress during this break. Do a little reading, take a walk, or chat with a neighbor. Think of it as a mini vacation.

You're giving yourself two gifts here. You're allowing your body and mind to refresh themselves, and you're also renewing that flush of excitement about your project as you return to it. Isn't the excitement more fun to feel than fatigue? And if you're quilting on some kind of deadline, don't worry—these short breaks won't make your project take longer! They'll actually help you stay more alert and quilt more efficiently.

The BRIC-A-BRAC QUILT

FINISHED BLOCK SIZE: 10½" X 10½"

FINISHED QUILT SIZE: 60" X 80"

DIANE: *"This is one visually textured quilt!"*

CHRISTINA: *"I was inspired by 'bric-a-brac,' a Victorian-era term for collections of elaborately decorative little items, clustered together on shelves, tables, or mantelpieces. This quilt, with its busy mixture of prints, has that same charming ornateness."*

DIANE: *"This quilt seems like a great exercise in developing color sense. You can start with one fabric you like, and then look closely at the print and pick out the specific colors in it. Then, look for other prints based on each of those colors."*

Skill Level:

SUPPLIES

Print 1: ¾ yard medium value
Print 2: ½ yard light value
Print 3: ¾ yard dark value
Print 4: ⅞ yard medium value
Print 5: ¾ yard dark value
Print 6: ⅞ yard light value
Print 7: 1¼ yards dark value
Backing: 3⅝ yards your choice of fabric
Binding: ½ yard your choice of fabric
Batting: 64" × 84"

FABRICS USED HERE

FreeSpirit: Habitat by Jay McCarroll

CUTTING THE FABRICS

Print 1: Cut 4 strips, 5½" × width of fabric.
Subcut them into 48 pieces, each measuring 3" × 5½".
Print 2: Cut 6 strips, 2¼" × width of fabric. Do not subcut them.
Print 3: Cut 6 strips, 3¾" × width of fabric. Do not subcut them.
Print 4: Cut 4 strips, 6¾" × width of fabric.
Subcut them into 48 pieces, each measuring 3" × 6¾".
Print 5: Cut 6 strips, 4" × width of fabric. Do not subcut them.
Print 6: Cut 6 strips, 4½" × width of fabric. Do not subcut them.
Print 7: Cut 4 strips, 10½" × width of fabric.
Subcut them into 48 pieces, each measuring 3" × 10½".

Christina's Tips

- The reason so many busy fabrics combine successfully in this quilt is that we've used an assortment of light, medium, and dark values. The lights and darks form an underlying pattern that unifies the prints.

- If the idea of finding so many coordinating prints feels intimidating, try choosing all your fabrics from the same designer's line. Fabrics in the same line generally have a unified set of colors.

ASSEMBLING THE QUILT BLOCKS

1. Sew a strip of Print 2 to a strip of Print 3 **(Diagram A)**, and press the seam allowance toward Print 3. Repeat this process with the remaining Print 2 and 3 strips, creating a total of six units. Square the left edge of each unit and then subcut it into eight pieces, each measuring $4^1/4'' \times 5^1/2''$. You should now have 48 units, which are called Print 2-3 .

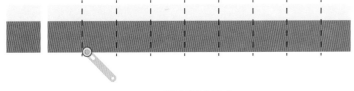

DIAGRAM A

2. Sew a strip of Print 5 to a strip of Print 6 **(Diagram B)**. Press the seam allowance toward Print 6. Repeat this process with the remaining Print 5 and 6 strips to create a total of six units. Square the left edge of each unit and then subcut it into eight pieces, each measuring $4^1/4'' \times 8''$. You should now have 48 units, which are called Print 5-6.

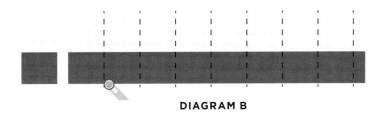

DIAGRAM B

3. Begin by assembling Block A, which appears at the edges of the quilt. Sew a Print 2-3 unit to a Print 1 piece, orienting them as shown in **Diagram C**. Press the seam allowance toward the Print 2-3 unit. Sew a Print 4 piece to the block, pressing the seam allowance toward Print 4.

4. Sew a Print 5-6 unit to the block, pressing the seam allowance toward the Print 5-6 unit. Sew a Print 7 piece to the block, pressing the seam allowance toward Print 7.

BLOCK A

DIAGRAM C

5. Repeat Steps 3 and 4 to assemble 16 Block As. The finished blocks should measure $10^1/2'' \times 10^1/2''$. Square them if necessary (see page 159).

6. Next, assemble Block B, which appears at the center of the quilt. (You may notice that Blocks A and B are mirror images of each other.) Begin by sewing a Print 2-3 unit to a Print 1 piece, orienting them as shown in **Diagram D**. Press the seam allowance toward the Print 2-3 unit. Next, sew a Print 4 piece to the block, pressing the seam allowance toward Print 4.

7. Sew a Print 5-6 unit to the block, pressing the seam allowance toward the Print 5-6 unit. Lastly, sew a Print 7 piece to the block, pressing the seam allowance toward Print 7.

8. Repeat Steps 6 and 7 to assemble 32 Block Bs. The finished blocks should measure $10^1/2'' \times 10^1/2''$. Square them if necessary.

BLOCK B

DIAGRAM D

ASSEMBLING THE QUILT TOP

9. Lay your finished blocks out in eight rows of six blocks each, using **Diagram E** for placement. Notice how the Block As have Print 7 facing toward the outer edges of the quilt and the Block Bs alternate in position, with Print 7 facing either the top or bottom.

DIAGRAM E

10. Sew the blocks of Row 1 together, nestling seams where they meet (see page 157). Press the seam allowances to one side. Repeat this process to assemble the other seven rows, pressing the seam allowances in alternating directions for each row.

11. Assemble the quilt top in sections. Sew Rows 1 through 4 together, nestling the seams. Press the seam allowances to one side, alternating the direction with each row.

12. Sew Rows 5 through 8 together in same manner. Then, sew the two sections together. Press the seam allowance to one side.

COMPLETED TOP

BACKING AND FINISHING

Make a 64" × 84" backing. Build a quilt sandwich and quilt. Cut eight 2" strips from your binding fabric and bind your quilt. (Refer to the Finishing Your Quilt section on page 159 as needed.)

- Stitch some big zigzags in a random pattern as we did on the sample quilt.
- Since this quilt has so many straight lines, a quilted pattern of loops or swirls would make a nice contrast.
- Simple stippling or straight lines in random widths would also look great!

Most of us know intuitively that quilting—or creating of any kind, really—is good for us. And occasionally, researchers enter the picture to document this fact more scientifically. The University of Glasgow conducted a study on the relationship between quilting and well-being in 2012, and after interviewing twenty-nine longtime quilters, concluded that:

"Color was psychologically uplifting. Quilting was challenging, demanded concentration and participants maintained and learned new skills. Participants experienced 'flow' while quilting. A strong social network fostered the formation of strong friendships. Affirmation from others boosted self-esteem and increased motivation for skill development. Quilts were often given altruistically and gave quilting added purpose."

Take out your quilting journal and ponder these questions.

- . . . So, what aspects of quilting make you happiest: The materials? The technical challenges? Meeting up with other quilters? Something else entirely?
- If you haven't quilted for a while, how do you feel?
- How much quilting do you need in your life? Do you need to spend a little time with your craft every day? Or do you immerse yourself in a project and then take a long break after it's finished?

As quilters, we all have specific colorways, prints, and shapes we love best—and there's nothing wrong with sticking to them most of the time. It's just that in your comfort zone, you tend to encounter fewer delightful creative surprises (which are so much fun)! Here are a few exercises to push your boundaries. Keep your quilt journal handy as you're doing them, so you can capture any epiphanies.

- Choose one quilt block design from this book that you just don't like that much. (It's okay, we won't be offended.) Now, make up this block in a selection of your very favorite fabrics. Does using colors and prints you love change the way you feel about the block?

- Choose a block design from this book that you love, but make it in colors you never use, or prints you wouldn't normally touch. (If you don't have any of these in your stash, consider doing this exercise with a quilting buddy and trading fabrics.) Were you able to see these fabrics in a new light as you worked with them? Did the design of the block give you any cues as to how these fabrics might play more nicely together?

- Choose a block design from this book and challenge yourself to come up with twelve color schemes for it, using only fabrics in your stash right now. You don't necessarily have to make all twelve blocks (unless you want to). You could just assemble twelve sets of fabric swatches. Which combinations were surprising to you? Try making the block out of those!

Think of it this way: The more you push yourself to try new things, the more creative tools you'll have at your disposal—and the more of those great "Eureka!" moments you'll get to enjoy.

CHAPTER 3

QUILTING *for* OTHERS

We all know that handmade quilts make beautiful, useful, and meaningful gifts. But have you ever thought about what happens in those hours you spend making that quilt? Some pretty powerful things are going on, actually: you're thinking kind thoughts about the people you're sewing for. You're spending these hours in the act of caring and giving. This is a mindset that has powerful effects on your own well-being, and it can actually strengthen your bond with the recipient of that quilt, even if you'll never meet him or her.

This chapter is all about the power of quilting for people you love and people you'd like to help. We'll share some quilt projects that make especially nice gifts, and some that work well as charity projects. We'll also explore tools to make your gift-quilting more organized and meaningful.

The TIME STANDS STILL QUILT

FINISHED BLOCK SIZE: 9" X 5"

FINISHED QUILT SIZE: 39" X 45"

CHRISTINA: *"This is one of my go-to gift quilts. The hourglass pattern is so simple that it looks lovely in both modern and traditional settings. You can render it bold and graphic or light and charming depending on your fabric choices."*

DIANE: *"It's what I call a timeless quilt! Those hourglasses also remind me of how time passes so quickly and yet so slowly when we're in the flow of creating. That's my favorite state of being!"*

Skill Level: ●●○

SUPPLIES

Background: 1 yard pin-dot print

Hourglasses: 1 fat quarter each of 10 coordinating prints

Backing: 1½ yards your choice of fabric

Binding: ½ yard your choice of fabric

Batting: 40" × 49" (crib/baby size)

FABRICS USED HERE

Sevenberry: Black Pin Dot

Moda Fabric: Sundae in Ruby by Bonnie & Camille

Lecien: Gingham in Yellow, Pink, and Green

Michael Miller: Mini Mikes Orange Tiny Gingham

Anthology Fabrics: Dream in Pink, The Woodlands by Khristian A. Howell

Yuwa of Japan: Kei Honeycomb Dot in Green

A few additional longtime stash fabrics

CUTTING THE FABRICS

Background/Black Pin Dot:

Cut 6 strips, 4¼" × width of fabric.

Subcut them into 40 pieces, each measuring 4¼" × 5¾".

Cut 5 strips, 1½" × width of fabric.

Subcut them into 18 pieces, each measuring 1½" × 9½".

Hourglasses/Prints (cut all pieces below from each print):

Cut 2 strips, 5½" × 22".

Subcut them into 4 pieces, each measuring 5½" × 10½".

ASSEMBLING THE QUILT BLOCKS

1. Pair up two $4^1/_4'' \times 5^3/_4''$ background pieces with *wrong* sides together, matching all edges. Cut them together on the diagonal. Repeat this process with the rest of the $4^1/_4'' \times 5^3/_4''$ background pieces. Keep these cut triangles in pairs with their wrong sides facing.

2. Place a $10^1/_2'' \times 5^1/_2''$ print piece on your work surface, right side up **(Diagram A)**. Measure $3^3/_8''$ in from each corner along the top edge, and use an erasable marking tool to mark the fabric at these locations. Line a ruler up with one of the marks and the bottom corner closest to it and cut. Repeat this process on the other side. Discard the triangles you've cut away or save them for another quilt.

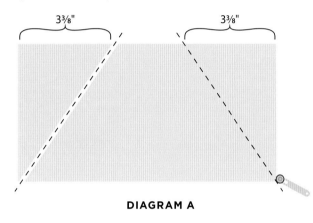

DIAGRAM A

3. Place one of the background triangles from Step 1 on top of the hourglass piece, with its bottom point matching the bottom of the hourglass. The background triangle will also extend a bit above the top edge of the hourglass **(Diagram B)**. Sew and press the seam allowance toward the hourglass. Sew the other background triangle to the opposite side of the hourglass in the same manner.

4. Repeat Steps 1 through 3 with the remaining $10^1/_2'' \times 5^1/_2''$ hourglass pieces. As you piece these half-blocks, press the seam allowances in alternating directions—toward the hourglass for one half-block and toward the background for the next.

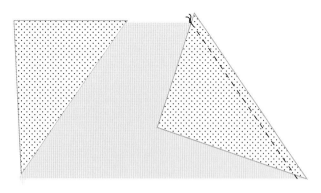

DIAGRAM B

5. Square these half-blocks, using the method below. After squaring, the two fabrics should meet right at the corners and the hourglass fabrics, at their narrowest points, should be exactly the same width. Take your time and make sure your alignments are correct before cutting.

   Place a half-block on your cutting mat, oriented as shown in **Diagram C**. Lay your ruler on top, aligning the narrow edge of the hourglass with the $5^1/_4''$ mark on the ruler. Now, slowly move your ruler to the left, maintaining this alignment, until you reach the point you see in the inset of **Diagram C**.

Christina's Tips

- Don't be too intimidated by the "experienced" skill level of this design. This is an unusual method of piecing—not particularly difficult, but it will require a little focus and patience at first.
- For this pattern, you'll need to mark your fabric before cutting it. We recommend using a FriXion pen, which erases with the heat of your iron.
- You'll find a $10^1/_2'' \times 10^1/_2''$ ruler useful for the precise squaring process we'll do in Step 5. Any larger square will work too, as long as it has measuring lines in $^1/_4''$ increments.

This point is actually where three points meet: the $\frac{1}{4}''$ line along the top edge of your ruler, the $9\frac{1}{4}''$ line on your ruler, and the edge of the hourglass fabric. If your alignment is correct here, then you should also see the edge of your background fabric lining up with the $9\frac{1}{2}''$ line on your ruler. Trim along the top and right edges of the half-block. Then, rotate it 180 degrees and finish squaring it to $9\frac{1}{2}'' \times 5''$. Repeat this step with all half-blocks.

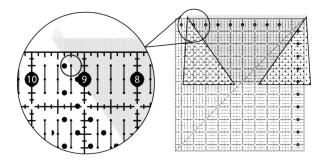

DIAGRAM C

6. Three rows of this quilt top will have a half hour-glass shape at each end. Choose the three prints you'd like to use for these end pieces and set aside two units of each, for a total of six. You'll use these when you assemble the quilt top.

7. Sort the rest of your half-blocks by print. Pair up two half-blocks of the same print that have their seam allowances pressed in opposite directions. Place them together with right sides facing, lining up the narrow edges of the print fabric. Nestle the seams and sew them together, pressing the seam allowance open (see page 157). Your finished blocks should resemble **Diagram D** and measure $9\frac{1}{2}'' \times 9\frac{1}{2}''$. Square them if necessary (see page 159).

DIAGRAM D

ASSEMBLING THE QUILT TOP

8. Decide how you'd like the prints arranged in your quilt top, using **Completed Top** for reference. The first row begins with a half-block **(Diagram E)**. Sew this block to a $1\frac{1}{2}'' \times 9\frac{1}{2}''$ background strip, pressing the seam allowance toward the strip.

Sew a full hourglass block to the background strip, pressing the seam allowances toward the background strip. Repeat this process, alternating strips and blocks, until your row contains three full blocks and a half-block at both ends. Assemble Row 3 and Row 5 in the same manner.

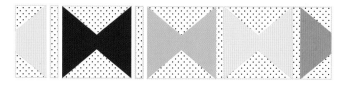

DIAGRAM E

9. To assemble Row 2 and Row 4, sew four blocks and three $1\frac{1}{2}'' \times 9\frac{1}{2}''$ background strips together, using **Diagram F** for placement. Press the seam allowances toward the background strips.

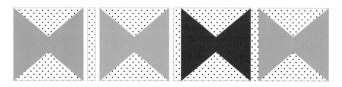

DIAGRAM F

10. Sew the rows together, pressing the seam allowances to one side or open.

COMPLETED TOP

BACKING AND FINISHING

Make a 40" × 49" backing. Build a quilt sandwich and quilt. Cut five 2" strips from your binding fabric and bind your quilt. (Refer to the Finishing Your Quilt section on page 159 as needed.)

Ideas for Quilting

- Outline stitch inside each of the hourglass blocks. Then, outline stitch inside each of the zigzag shapes created between the hourglasses.
- Stitch big and small swirls all over the top, which is a nice way to contrast with the straight-line pattern.
- Try quilting clouds, moving from one cloud to the next with continuous line quilting.

MAKE A GIFT-GIVING PLANNER

In Chapters 1 and 2, we talked about the many ways your quilt journal can help you explore your creativity. Here's another journal-like project that can help you create all those quilts you want to make for other people. Start with a blank book of some kind—or an index card file, or some notes you can access on your smart phone. Whatever format feels most useful to you is the right format here.

Next, designate a page (or card, or whatever) for each person on your gift list. Write their name, and if it inspires you, paste in a picture of them, too. Write down any important gift-giving dates: their birthday, anniversary, graduation date, baby due dates—more than likely, you'll keep updating this list over time. Then, start compiling notes on what they like and don't like. When you visit their homes (or see pictures), make note of what colors, textures, and ideas you see there. (Make note of the bed sizes in their homes, too!)

While you're at it, notice what colors and styles they wear most, and either jot down notes or paste in more pictures. You might even want to make note of their height (that could be helpful information in planning a lap quilt). If you happen across a quilt pattern they might like, sketch it or paste in a photo. Carry your gift planner with you when you go to the fabric store. If you see a fabric you think might work for someone on your list, you'll have all the visual references you need to make sure it's the right choice. And if you buy some fabric to stash away for their quilt, tape swatches onto their page so you don't forget.

Gift quilts (as we well know) require planning, design choices, and hours of making. A journal like this one can be a huge help in keeping your ideas and supplies organized so that when the time comes, you'll be able to make something that fits your recipient's lifestyle perfectly.

The GENEVA QUILT

FINISHED BLOCK SIZE: 11" X 11"
FINISHED QUILT SIZE: 60" X 75"

CHRISTINA: *"I'm a fan of the two-color quilt, because it's an exercise in subtlety. On the surface, this looks like white crosses on a red background, but look closer. The fabrics have texture, and the seams create another pattern on top of that. There's really a lot happening beneath the surface."*

DIANE: *"This design would make a lovely charity quilt, because it's simple, straight seam piecing, it lends itself to a lot of different fabrics, and I just like the positivity of all these plusses!"*

Skill Level:

SUPPLIES
Background: 3¾ yards red solid
Pluses: ¾ yard white solid
Backing: 3¾ yards your choice of fabric
Binding: ½ yard your choice of fabric
Batting: 64" × 79" (twin size)

FABRICS USED HERE
Moda Cross Weave: Scarlet
Moda Bella Solid: White

CUTTING THE FABRICS
Background/Red Solid:
Cut 8 strips, 2½" × width of fabric. Do not subcut them.
Cut 11 strips, 7" × width of fabric.
Subcut them into 64 squares, each measuring 7" × 7".
Subcut these squares on the diagonal, creating 128 half square triangles.
Cut 3 strips, 11" × width of fabric.
Subcut them into 8 squares, each measuring 11" × 11".
Subcut 7 of these squares on the diagonal, creating 14 half square triangles.
Subcut 1 of these squares on both diagonals, creating 4 quarter square triangles.

Pluses/White Solid:
Cut 4 strips, 2½" × width of fabric. Do not subcut them.
Cut 2 strips, 6½" × width of fabric.
Subcut them into 32 pieces, each measuring 2½" × 6½".

Christina's Tips

- Half square triangles create a lot of bias-oriented fabric, which is a bit stretchy and can pucker at seams (particularly with the cross-weave fabrics used in the sample quilt). Pin all seams before sewing and you'll have a smoother result.

- If you've never hand quilted, this is a good quilt to try it out on, especially if you're using cross-weave fabrics: their loose weave makes it easier to move the needle in and out.

ASSEMBLING THE QUILT BLOCKS

1. Sew a 2½" red strip to each side of a 2½" white strip **(Diagram A)**. Press the seam allowances toward the white strip. Repeat this process with the rest of the 2½" strips, creating four red-white-red strip units. Square the left edge of each unit and then subcut it into 16 pieces, each measuring 2½" × 6½". You should now have a total of 64 pieces.

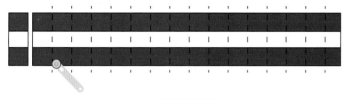

DIAGRAM A

2. Sew a red-white-red strip unit to either side of a white 2½" × 6½" strip **(Diagram B)**. Press the seam allowances toward the white strip. Repeat this process with the rest of the units from Step 1, creating a total of 32 "plus" squares.

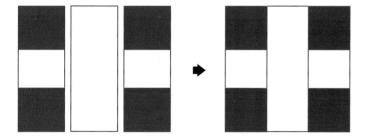

DIAGRAM B

3. Orient a "plus" square as shown in **Diagram C**, with the long white strip being horizontal. Sew a 7" half square triangle to the right and left edges of this square, taking care to center them. (See page 154 for a centering trick.) Press the seam allowances toward the "plus" square. Trim the excess fabric at the top and bottom of each triangle flush with the square. Repeat this process for all 32 "plus" squares.

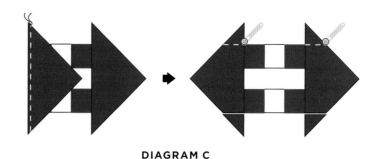

DIAGRAM C

4. Sew a 7" half square triangle to the other two sides of the square **(Diagram D)**. Press the seam allowances toward the center. Repeat this process to create 32 finished blocks.

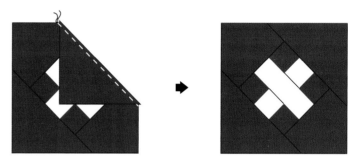

DIAGRAM D

ASSEMBLING THE QUILT TOP

Assemble this quilt in diagonal rows, using **Diagram E** for placement. Pay careful attention to how the seams within each block are oriented.

5. To begin the first row, orient a block as shown in Row 1 of **Diagram E**. Sew an 11" quarter square triangle to the top edge of the block and press the seam allowance toward the quarter square triangle. Next, sew an 11" half square triangle to either side of the block, pressing the seam allowances toward the center block.

   This step forms the top right corner of your quilt. Repeat this step to create the bottom left corner, also known as Row 8.

6. Follow **Diagram E** for steps 6–8. Alternate the direction of the plus blocks from row to row as shown in the **Completed Top**. Sew three blocks together for Row 2. Press the seam allowances away from the center block. Sew an 11″ half square triangle to each end of the row. Press the seam allowances toward the center of the strip. Repeat this process to create Row 7.

7. Sew five blocks together for Row 3. Press the seam allowances of the center block toward the center of the row, and the rest of the seam allowances away from the center of the row. Sew an 11″ half square triangle to each end of the row, pressing the seam allowances toward the center of the row. Repeat this process to create Row 6.

8. Sew seven blocks together for Row 4. Press the seam allowances of the center block *away* from the center of the row, and the rest of the seam allowances *toward* the center of the row.

Sew an 11″ quarter square triangle to the left end of the row, pressing the seam allowance toward the center of the row. Sew an 11″ half square triangle to the right end of the row, pressing the seam allowance toward the center of the row. Repeat this process to create Row 5.

9. Sew Rows 1 through 4 together, taking care to nestle the seams (see page 157). Press the row seam allowances to one side, alternating the direction for each row. Sew Rows 5 through 8 together in the same manner to create a separate section.

10. Rotate Rows 5 through 8 180 degrees, referring to **Diagram E**. Sew the two sections together and press the seam allowance to one side.

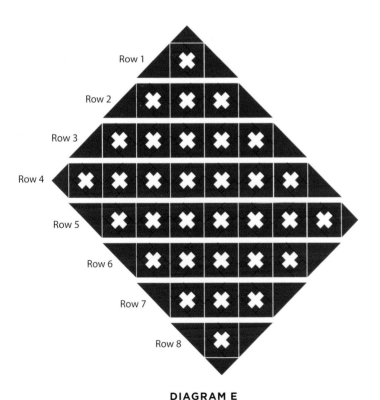

DIAGRAM E

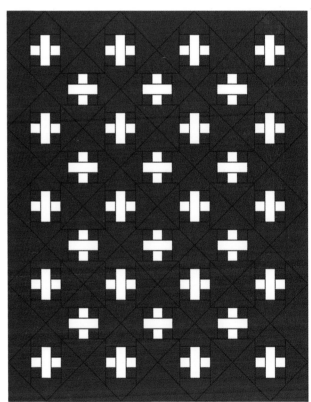

COMPLETED TOP

BACKING AND FINISHING

Make a 64" × 79" backing. Build a quilt sandwich and quilt. Cut seven 2" strips from your binding fabric and bind your quilt. (Refer to the Finishing Your Quilt section on page 159 as needed.)

Ideas for Quilting

- The sample quilt is hand quilted with simple lines around the plus shapes, which are rendered in a chunky running stitch using embroidery floss. This is minimal quilting; it does its job of keeping the layers together, but leaves the quilt soft and with lots of drape.
- Try quilting in the negative space, echoing the lines of the blocks.
- Crosshatching would be a great, simple quilting pattern for this design.

Creative Exercise:
WORDS OF LOVE

Chances are, anyone on your gift quilt list has a favorite word or phrase of some kind—whether it's an inspirational quote, a catchphrase she uses all the time, or perhaps the shiny new name of a newborn baby. How might you add these words to the quilt you're making?

You can always embroider text on your quilts, using a water-soluble marker to draw the letters onto the fabric first. You can also find letter stencils at most craft stores, which, combined with fabric paints, are an easy way to add words. We now have fabrics that will pass through a laser printer (see the Resources section), so you can create a custom label or appliqué. There's even a genre of "word quilts," on which quilters are forming words by piecing fabric into letter blocks. (Want to learn more about this? An online search for "word quilts" will bring you lots of resources.)

So here's a creative exercise for the next quilted gift you make: Ask yourself what words best represent your recipient. Look at the quilt you're planning and find a space where you can tuck these words into the design. Now, how will you paint, stitch, or print them?

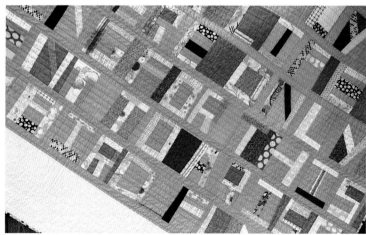

Tools for Happiness:
CHARITY QUILTING KIT

If you've been wanting to make some quilts for local charities, but just can't seem to find the time or figure out the right project, try making yourself a Charity Quilting Kit. All you need is a medium-size box with a lid. (Office supply stores sell "banker's boxes" that work beautifully.) If you want to be fancy about things, cover your box with some fabric or contact paper. Glue a 9" x 12" envelope to the lid of this box and you're all set.

Next, it's time to supply this Charity Quilting Kit. We all seem to end up with fabrics in our stashes that we don't plan to use, but don't want to toss. When these fabrics drift into your life, put them in your box! The next time you buy batting for a quilt project, buy some extra for charity projects and file it away in your box as well. And any time you run across a quilt pattern you think would work well for charity projects, print or photocopy it and file it in the envelope.

There's a certain magic in the simple act of keeping all your charity quilting supplies in one dedicated place. Once you have everything accumulated, you'll find it much easier to get started. And here's an interesting side effect of this process: Since you're collecting fabrics for this Charity Quilting Kit rather haphazardly over time, you're bound to find some interesting, creativity-stretching challenges as you combine the colors and prints into quilts.

If you want to join a charity quilting group, you'll find some good ones in the Resources section.

The HAPHAZARD CHEVRON PILLOW

FINISHED PROJECT SIZE: 12" SQUARE

CHRISTINA: *"Sometimes, I want to quilt a gift for someone but it doesn't make sense to create a full-size quilt. That's when I turn to this pillow. You can change its look by changing the fabrics; subtle prints create a whole other effect than the solids I've used here. It's a nice sort of blank canvas for customizing to the person I'm quilting for."*

DIANE: *"With this fairly improvisational piecing, too, each pillow you make is one of a kind. That's a nice gift-giving touch."*

Skill Level:

SUPPLIES

Pillow Top Fabric: ½ yard each
 of two contrasting fabrics
Backing Fabric: 1 fat quarter of
 coordinating print
Muslin/Lining Fabric: ½ yard
Batting: 2 pieces, each
 measuring 12½" × 12½"
Pillow Form: 12" × 12"

FABRICS USED HERE

FreeSpirit Designer Solids:
 Arctic White
Robert Kaufman Kona Solid:
 Black

CUTTING THE FABRICS

Pillow Top Fabrics (cut as outlined below for each fabric):
Cut the selvage off, rotate the
 piece 180 degrees, and cut
 off the fold of the yardage.
 You'll have 2 pieces, each
 measuring approximately
 18" × 22". Leave them
 stacked together with
 wrong sides facing.
Muslin/Lining Fabric: Cut 2
 squares, 12½" × 12½".
Backing: Cut 1 square,
 12½" × 12½".

Christina's Tips

- Instead of using only two fabrics for the pillow top, try incorporating some print strips in the same colorway. Go for subtle prints that add a bit of interest but still maintain a striking color contrast overall.
- Incidentally, when you do the initial cuts on your yardage for this project, you end up with 18" × 22" pieces, which is fat quarter size. So you could always purchase two fat quarters of either fabric instead of yardage.
- You'll find a 6" × 24" (or larger) ruler handy for this project, since you'll be making a number of fairly long cuts. Just make sure it has a 45-degree-angle line.

ASSEMBLING THE PILLOW TOP

1. Work with your darker fabric first, with both 18" × 22" pieces stacked together (wrong sides facing). Cut the stack into strips of various widths, between 1" × 22" and 3" × 22". You decide what combination of widths to use—just make sure that together, they total about 10". (The sample pillow used these widths: 3", 1½", 2", 1", and 2½".) The reason the total width is important is that you'll need this much to create a 12" height for the pillow.

   Since you're cutting through two layers of fabric, you'll have two pieces of each width. So, separate the strips into two identical piles. Repeat this process with your lighter fabric. You should now have four piles of strips: two lighter and two darker.

2. Working with one pile of darker strips and one pile of lighter strips, sew them together, alternating the color and varying the widths **(Diagram A)**. Press the seam allowances toward the darker fabric strips. If the top and bottom edges of this unit are uneven, square them (see page 159). Repeat this process with the remaining piles of light and dark strips, arranging them as you like, to create a second unit.

DIAGRAM A

3. Place one of these units on your cutting surface. Lay your ruler on top, aligning its 45-degree-angle line with the bottom edge of the unit **(Diagram B)**.

Your first cut should be 13" long, so slide your ruler to one side until the measurement lines on the right edge show that you have 13" of space between the bottom and right edges of the unit. Cut here to remove a corner of the unit and discard it.

4. Rotate the unit so that the newly cut edge is vertical and facing left. Align the cut edge and your ruler with a vertical line on your cutting surface. Now, cut the unit into several strips, with widths between 2" and 3" (varying the widths as you like). Narrower strips here will create a more visually complex pillow. Wider strips will create a bolder one.

   Keep cutting until you get to the other corner of the unit, and stop cutting once your strips fall below 13" long.

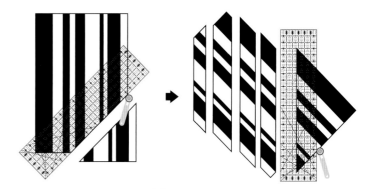

DIAGRAM B

5. Repeat Steps 3 and 4 with the second strip unit, but this time, rotate the ruler so it's angled 45 degrees in the opposite direction **(Diagram C)**. Align the 45-degree line on your ruler with the top edge of the unit. Start cutting at the right side of the unit with a 13" cut. Then rotate the unit so the newly cut edge is vertical and facing left, and cut strips of varying widths.

6. Arrange the cut strips on your cutting surface, alternating strips from each set to create chevrons **(Diagram D)**. Keep the strips aligned with the vertical guides on your cutting surface, and keep add-

DIAGRAM E

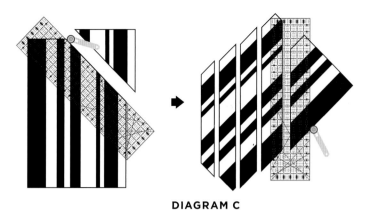

DIAGRAM C

ing strips until the overall width is roughly 18". The strips will be of different lengths, so do your best to keep them roughly centered to one another. The finished piece should be at least 13" tall, so make sure your strips are positioned to allow that. Trim the top and bottom edges of the strips square.

DIAGRAM D

7. Sew the strips together. Because these strips were cut on the bias, they can stretch, so pin them before you sew to minimize stretch. Press each seam allowance open. Trim the finished pillow top to $12\frac{1}{2}$" × $12\frac{1}{2}$".

ASSEMBLING THE PILLOW

8. Layer the pillow top with one batting piece and quilt it as you like. (The sample pillow is quilted $\frac{1}{4}$" on either side of the vertical seams.) Place a muslin square on the back of the pillow top and baste the layers together around all four sides **(Diagram E)**.

9. Make a second quilt sandwich for the back of the pillow: layer the backing square with the second piece of batting and the other piece of muslin and baste them together around all four sides. Don't quilt this piece.

   Pin the pillow front and back together with right sides facing. Sew around the edges with a $\frac{1}{4}$" seam allowance, leaving a 9" opening at the bottom for stuffing **(Diagram F)**. Trim all four corners at a 45-degree angle. Now, turn the pillowcase right side out, using a pencil or ruler to push the corners out from the inside.

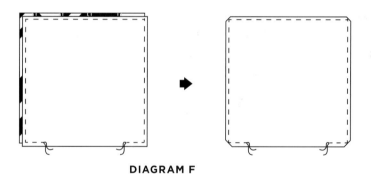

DIAGRAM F

10. Press all four sides of the pillow, especially at the opening. Make sure the raw edges at the opening are turned in $\frac{1}{4}$". Stuff the pillowcase with a pillow form, gently pushing the corners of the form into the case and making sure the form is evenly distributed. Sew the opening closed with a ladder stitch (see page 155).

Kay Bailey started making quilts somewhat by accident. Back in 2006, she was planning her wedding and decided to ask friends and family to send her small, meaningful trinkets that she could sew into her wedding dress.

"It was going to symbolize how our 'tribes' and all of our respective stories were now becoming united through this marriage," she says. But before long, the project got a bit unwieldy. "I eventually got so many contributions that they were too heavy to put on a piece of clothing. So I put them on a wall hanging quilt instead. Each bauble had its own five-inch square, and I made a booklet that went along with it, indicating the person who had contributed each piece and the story that went with it."

That quilt sparked a new calling for Kay—a small business called Fiber of Her Being. Now she makes custom quilts and pillows to help people mark milestones, cope with illness, or remember lost loved ones. Kay shared the challenges and rewards of this work.

What's it like to make these deeply meaningful pieces for people who, in some cases, you haven't even met in person?

When I make personalized quilts for people, they provide the story. Only after I've talked to them and found out not just what pictures or colors I should include, but what the feeling is that I should invoke, and what purpose the quilt or pillow will have, can I start. When I'm making it, I think about the recipients and their families the entire time. By the time I have finished the project, I feel like I am a part of the family, and I find that I have really come to love them . . . even if I have never met them.

How did you get involved in making quilted pillows for people going through illness?

My friend Paul suggested the idea of Chemo Pillows (which later became Comfort Pillows and Comfort Quilts) when his mother was going through chemo. Her name was Margit Bollyky. She had been practically a surrogate mother for me while I was in college, and I loved her deeply. I made the pillow with pictures of her grandchildren (and grand-dog), and I could imagine her taking it with her to the chemo treatments. Paul said that it provided not only physical comfort but also emotional comfort, because she could see the pictures of the people she was going through this for, and knew that Paul and I had come up with the idea and pillow just for her. After Margit passed away, I started making Comfort items for people undergoing surgery or some other physical difficulty, or people going through some emotional difficulty like the death of a loved one. The more personal or traumatic their story, the more I feel it is my life's work to offer comfort to these people (these strangers that I come to love while I make them their quilts).

It seems like being immersed in all these sad stories would begin to affect you after a while. Do you make any quilts commemorating happy occasions?
I do make another kind of sentimental quilt: T-shirt quilts. These are usually happy things that people order to be made from their own T-shirt collections as a present for themselves, or out of their spouse's collections—both as a present and often to help clean out the closet or basement. I have done several T-shirt quilts for people who are about to have their first child and need to open up some space in their home that the shirts currently occupy.

I have also done a number of T-shirt quilts for sports players who collect shirts from every team they have played on, and for runners who get a shirt with every race. One of my clients had her running shirts made into a wall hanging to celebrate her accomplishment of having lost one hundred pounds through the running. Another woman had grown up all around the world (her parents were in the foreign service) and said that because she didn't have a place that she could call home, her T-shirt collection served as her home. It was a constant that she could build on as she moved every year or two. That was very poignant.

Does it feel different, working on a quilt you're making for a joyous occasion like a wedding, versus making a quilt that's designed to comfort someone who is grieving a loss?
Yes. Yes, yes, yes! I have a range of feelings as I make these things. First of all, the more pictures or pieces of clothing I get from the customer, the more interesting the project is to me, because the closer it is to the lives of the people involved. I am happy to help commemorate or celebrate a happy occasion, but there is no question that the work I do to comfort people—while they face health issues, or are left to come to terms with a death—is much, much more touching for me. It is there that I feel that my talents are truly being used to help the world. It's a particular kind of contribution that not everybody can make.

Why quilts? Why do they make such a good carrier for your clients' life stories?
Quilts (and pillows) are art that you can use, and that physically provides warmth and softness. Then I can use the materials that belong (or belonged) to someone, which makes the product that much more personal. Like letters that you send through the mail, you know these pieces of material were actually touched by, or earned by, or collected by you or someone you loved. Finally, add to that the fact that I can print photographs or text onto fabric and work those images and thoughts into the whole. And then you can't *help* but have the thing be emotional!

The STARSTRUCK QUILT

FINISHED BLOCK SIZE: THIS QUILT IS ASSEMBLED IN ROWS
RATHER THAN BLOCKS.
FINISHED QUILT SIZE: 64" X 88"

CHRISTINA: *"This quilt started with a simple, almost meditative process of laying shapes over shapes . . . which then created shapes within shapes, and that led to this combination of stars and squares. I love the surprises that emerge when you play with forms."*

DIANE: *"If I were making this quilt as a gift, I'd use the central squares as 'showcase spots' for my recipient's favorite fabrics."*

Skill Level:

SUPPLIES
Background: 3½ yards gray solid
Star Points: 2½ yards blue solid
Star Centers: ½ yard each of four
    coordinating prints
Backing: 5¼ yards your choice of
    fabric
Binding: ½ yard your choice of
    fabric

FABRICS USED HERE:
Michael Miller Fabrics: Sanctuary
    by Patty Young, Glass Tiles, and
    Zen Garden
Blank Quilting: Egg Dots by Hoodie
FreeSpirit Fabrics: Zoo Menagerie
    by Eleanor Grosch
Robert Kaufman Kona Cotton: Coal,
    Marine

CUTTING THE FABRICS
Background/Gray Solid:
Cut 9 strips, 7¼" × width of fabric.
Subcut them into 41 squares, each
    measuring 7¼" × 7¼".
Cut 4 strips, 4¼" × width of fabric.
Subcut them into 34 squares, each
    measuring 4¼" × 4¼".
Cut 6 strips, 4½" × width of fabric.
Subcut them into 48 squares, each
    measuring 4½" × 4½".
Cut 5 strips, 2½" × width of fabric.
Subcut them into 68 squares, each
    measuring 2½" × 2½".

Star Points/Blue Solid:
Cut 9 strips, 7¼" × width of fabric.
Subcut them into 41 squares, each
    measuring 7¼" × 7¼".
Cut 4 strips, 4½" × width of fabric.
Subcut them into 34 squares, each
    measuring 4½" × 4½".

Star Centers/Prints (cut all pieces below from each print):
Cut 2 strips, 4½" × width of fabric.
Subcut them into 48 squares, each
    measuring 4½" × 4½".
Cut 2 strips, 2½" × width of fabric.
Subcut them into 68 squares, each
    measuring 2½" × 2½".

Christina's Tips

- There are many points
  in this quilt where lots
  of pieces of fabric come
  together. Follow the
  pressing instructions in
  this project carefully to
  minimize bulk.

ASSEMBLING THE QUILT BLOCKS

We'll refer to Half Square Triangles as HSTs. For details on how to assemble them, see page 155.

1. Use one gray and one blue $7\frac{1}{4}$″ square to make four HSTs. Press the seam allowances toward the gray fabric. Repeat this process with the rest of the $7\frac{1}{4}$″ squares, creating a total of 164 HSTs. Square each HST to $4\frac{1}{2}$″ × $4\frac{1}{2}$″ (see page 159).

Repeat this process with the $4\frac{1}{4}$″ gray and blue squares, creating a total of 136 HSTs. Square each of these HSTs to $2\frac{1}{2}$″ × $2\frac{1}{2}$″.

2. Sew these squares into pairs **(Diagram A)** so they form the points of the stars. With the blue star points facing away from you, press the seam allowance to the left. Repeat this step with the rest of the $4\frac{1}{2}$″ and $2\frac{1}{2}$″ HSTs, creating a total of 82 larger and 78 smaller pairs.

3. Now, work with the four prints that make up the star centers. We'll call these A, B, C, and D. Sew Print A to Print B and press the seam allowance toward Print A. Sew Print C to Print D and press the seam allowance toward Print C. Sew these two units together **(Diagram B)**. Clip into the seam allowance (see page 158). Press seam allowance A toward D, and press seam allowance C toward B.

Repeat this process with the rest of the $4\frac{1}{2}$″ and all of the $2\frac{1}{2}$″ print squares. Square all of these units. The larger ones should measure $8\frac{1}{2}$″ × $8\frac{1}{2}$″ and the smaller ones should measure $4\frac{1}{2}$″ × $4\frac{1}{2}$″.

4. Set six of the assembled $8\frac{1}{2}$″ print squares aside for now. Use the remaining print squares to make large stars. Orient the print square as shown in **Diagram C**. Sew an HST pair to the top and bottom edges of the print square. Press the seam allowances toward the print square.

Next, sew two $4\frac{1}{2}$″ gray/background squares to opposite ends of two HST pairs. Press the

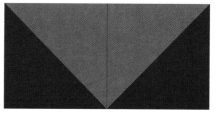

FRONT

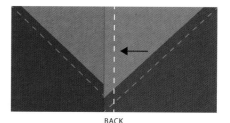

BACK

DIAGRAM A

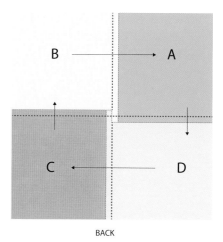

BACK

FRONT

DIAGRAM B

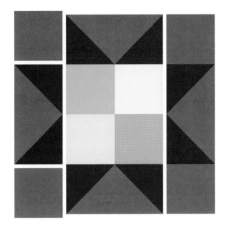

DIAGRAM C

SET A

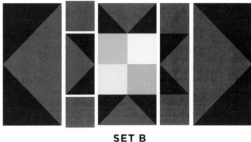

SET B

DIAGRAM D

seam allowances toward the gray squares. Sew these units to the right and left edges of the print square. Press the seam allowances toward the prints. Repeat this process to make 12 large stars. Square them to $16\frac{1}{2}" \times 16\frac{1}{2}"$.

5. Assemble the smaller stars in two groups, using **Diagram D** as a guide. First, sew a pair of HST units to the right and left edges of the print square. Press the seam allowances toward the print square. Sew two $2\frac{1}{2}"$ gray squares to opposite ends of two more HST pairs, pressing the seam allowances toward the gray squares. Sew these units to the top and bottom edges of the print square, pressing the seam allowances toward the prints. Repeat this process to make eight units, which are Small Star A.

6. For the remaining nine small stars, you'll work in reverse so the seam allowances can lie flatter. Sew a pair of HSTs to the top and bottom edges of a print square. Press the seam allowances toward the prints. Sew two $2\frac{1}{2}"$ gray background squares to opposite ends of two more HST pairs. Press the seam allowances toward the gray squares. Sew these units to the right and left edges of the print

square, pressing the seam allowances toward the prints. Repeat this process to make nine Small Star Bs. Square these blocks to $8\frac{1}{2}" \times 8\frac{1}{2}"$.

7. Now, add extensions to the Small Star A units by sewing a larger HST pair to the top and bottom edges of the star **(Diagram D)**. Press the seam allowances toward the star center.

For the Small Star B units, sew the larger HST pairs to the right and left edges of the star. Press the seam allowances away from the star center.

ASSEMBLING THE QUILT TOP

8. Use **Diagram E** for this step. There are two row styles in this quilt: Row A contains the large star blocks and Small Star A units, and Row B contains Small Star B units alternating with those leftover print squares from Step 4.

Assemble four Row As, pressing the seam allowances toward the large stars. Assemble three Row Bs, pressing the seam allowances toward the large print blocks.

9. Sew the rows together, alternating them as in **Diagram E**. Press the row seam allowances open.

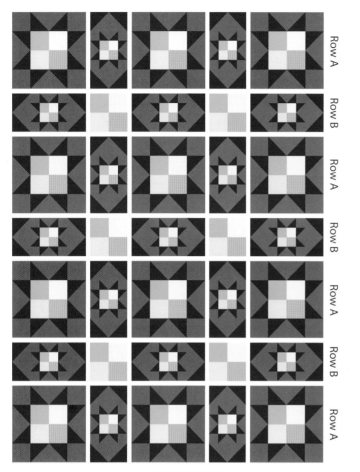

Row A
Row B
Row A
Row B
Row A
Row B
Row A

DIAGRAM E

COMPLETED TOP

BACKING AND FINISHING

10. Make a 68″ × 92″ backing. Build a quilt sandwich and quilt. Cut eight 2″ strips from your binding fabric and bind your quilt. (Refer to the Finishing Your Quilt section on page 159 as needed.)

Ideas for Quilting

- Swirls would give a fantastic celestial feel to all of the stars of this quilt.
- For a simple but effective quilting pattern, try quilting around the outside edge of the big and small stars.
- With so many half square triangles in this design, a pattern of diagonal lines across the quilt would be a harmonious choice.

Creative Exercise:

DESIGNING IT TOGETHER

When you set out to give someone a handmade quilt, you're also giving them a significant gift of your time and energy. You hope that the quilt will be used often and cherished forever. But after all, a quilt is also a large decorative presence in a home, and everyone has definite ideas about what feels beautiful and comfortable. So when you're planning to make a quilt for someone special, why not involve them in the process of designing it? That way, you'll know that the hours you spend sewing will result in a quilt they'll love to have in their home, and you'll have some fun times together. Here are some ways you can involve them in the process:

- Spend an afternoon tea time with them, looking through quilt pattern books, magazines, and websites. Ask them to make notes on the quilts they like best and why. Share some designs you were thinking of quilting— what are their impressions? Do they already have any quilts in their home? What do they like most about them?

- Visit their house and have them show you where they'll use the quilt. Ask them what their favorite objects are in that room and why they chose the colors they're using in their decor. Use this information to work out a color palette with them. If you can, collect some paint chips or magazine clippings to represent these colors.

- Take them to your favorite quilt store to look at fabrics, and take along those color references. Try to schedule this visit at a nice, relaxed time, so you can give them lots of space to overcome any intimidation they might be feeling about this step. Let them choose a stack of bolts they like, and then help them refine these into a nice balance of prints and solids.

If you want to retain some elements of surprise in your gift, you could always keep it a secret which fabrics you'll use for which parts of the design, or what method you'll use to quilt it, or how you'll piece the backing. Once the quilt is finished, your gift recipient will value it even more because now they'll have a clearer picture of what went into its creation.

The PETAL PIE QUILT

FINISHED BLOCK SIZE: 15½" X 15½"

FINISHED QUILT SIZE: 49" X 49"

CHRISTINA: *"This quilt came about while I was playing with a traditional block called Drunkard's Path. It's a seemingly simple block, really just a quarter circle on a background. But when you make it in multiples and move them around, you end up with some beautiful shapes."*

DIANE: *"I could see this as a wonderful gift quilt for a little (or big) girl's room. In fact, would you like to make me one?"*

Skill Level:

SUPPLIES

Background: 3 yards white solid
Flowers: ⅝ yard each of five prints
Backing: 3 yards your choice of fabric
Binding: ⅜ yard your choice of fabric
Batting: 54" × 54" (throw/twin)
Templates A and B (located on page 172)

FABRICS USED HERE

Daisy Janie Organic Fabrics: Tilly by Jan DiCintio
FreeSpirit Designer Solids: Arctic White

CUTTING THE FABRICS

Background/White Solid:

See page 154 for more on cutting sashing and border strips.

Cut 2 strips, 2½" × *length* of fabric.

Subcut them into 4 lengths, 2 measuring 2½" × 45½" and 2 measuring 2½" × 49½".

Cut 36 squares, each measuring 9¾" × 9¾", from the remaining fabric.

Flowers/Prints:

From four of your prints, cut 2 strips each, 9½" × width of fabric.

Subcut these into 8 squares, each measuring 9½" × 9½".

From the remaining print, cut 1 strip, 9½" × width of fabric.

Subcut this into 4 squares, each measuring 9½" × 9½". (See the Tips at right.)

Christina's Tips

- After you cut the strip from your fifth piece of print fabric, you should have just enough left over to use for binding. That's assuming you didn't have to square the edges of your yardage too much before cutting.

- A 4½" square ruler (or larger) comes in handy for squaring the Drunkard's Path units.

ASSEMBLING THE QUILT BLOCKS

You'll first assemble 16 Drunkard's Path units, and then sew them together into the larger flower motif block.

1. Start with four squares of the same print, and fold them into quarters with wrong sides facing, making sure all raw edges are aligned. Lightly press the folds. Place Template A onto one folded square, lining up the straight edges of the template with the raw edges of the fabric. Using a rotary cutter, cut around the curve of the template through all four layers **(Diagram A)**. Repeat this process with the other three squares to create a total of 16 Template A pieces.

2. Fold four background squares into quarters with wrong sides facing, lining up all raw edges. Lightly press the folds. Place Template B onto one folded square, lining up the straight edges of the template with the raw edges of the fabric. Cut around the ends and curve of the template through all layers with a rotary cutter **(Diagram A)**. Repeat this process with the three remaining background squares to create a total of 16 Template B pieces.

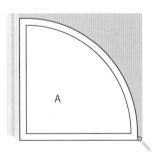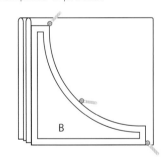

DIAGRAM A

3. Pin one Template A print and a Template B solid as shown in **Diagram B**. (See page 156 for more on working with curves.) Sew around the curve with a $1/4$″ seam allowance. Press the seam allowance toward the print. Repeat this process with the remaining Template A and Template B pieces to create 16 Drunkard's Path units.

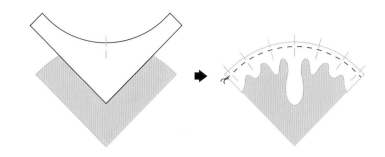

DIAGRAM B

4. To square this unit, place it on your cutting mat, orienting it as shown in **Diagram C**. Lay a square ruler on top, lining up the $1/4$″ measurement lines at the top and right edges of the ruler with the very edges of the print curve. (You'll want to have only $1/4$″ of background fabric at the top and right edges of the unit so that the edges of the curves will meet precisely when sewn together.) Trim the top and right edges of the unit and then rotate it 180 degrees. Trim it to $4\frac{1}{4}$″ × $4\frac{1}{4}$″. Repeat this process with the remaining units.

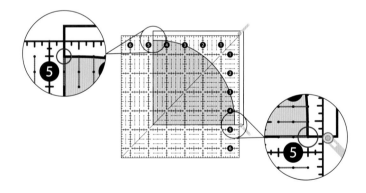

DIAGRAM C

5. Sew these units together in pairs, orienting them as you see in **Diagram D**. Press the seam allowance toward the print. Repeat this process to create a total of eight units.

   Note: If, as you're sewing the units together, you happen to sew through the curved edge at the top, don't worry too much about it if it's within the top

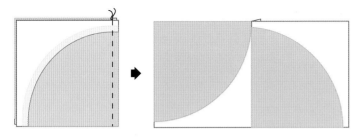

DIAGRAM D

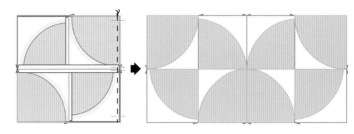

DIAGRAM F

1/4" of the seam. Since these units will be sewn to others as the top progresses, that portion will be hidden in a seam allowance and no one will ever know.

6. Next sew two of these double units together, rotating the second one 180 degrees from the first as shown in **Diagram E**. You'll have two seams meeting up in the center, so nestle them together (see page 157). Press the seam allowances open. Repeat this process three more times to create a total of four petal units.

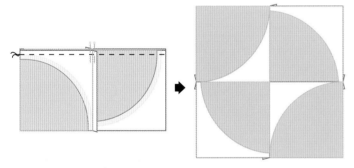

DIAGRAM E

7. Place two petal units together with right sides facing, orienting them as shown in **Diagram F**. Match the pressed-open seams at the center of each petal together, pinning at both sides of the seam allowance. Sew the petals together and press the seam allowance open. Repeat this process with the second set of petals.

8. Place the two petal sets together, orienting them as shown in **Diagram G**. Nestle the pressed-open seams. Sew them together and press the seam allowance open. Your finished block should measure 15½" × 15½".

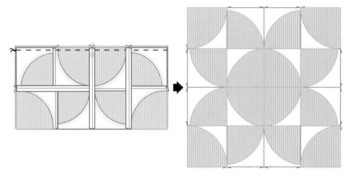

DIAGRAM G

9. Repeat Steps 1 through 8 eight more times to create a total of nine flower blocks.

ASSEMBLING THE QUILT TOP

10. Lay your flower blocks out in three rows of three blocks each, arranging the colors as you like and using **Completed Top** as a reference. If you've decided to use the leftover fabric from your fifth print for your binding, place the flower made from this print at the center.

Sew the flower blocks together in rows, nestling all seams. Press all seam allowances open.

11. Sew the three rows together, pressing the seam allowances open.

12. Add skinny borders to help frame the quilt top. Sew a $2\frac{1}{2}" \times 45\frac{1}{2}"$ strip to the right and left edges of the top, pressing the seam allowances toward the quilt top. Next, sew a $2\frac{1}{2}" \times 49\frac{1}{2}"$ strip to the top and bottom edges of the quilt top. Press the seam allowances toward the quilt top.

BACKING AND FINISHING

Make a 54" × 54" backing. Build a quilt sandwich and quilt. Cut six 2" strips from your binding fabric and bind your quilt. (Refer to the Finishing Your Quilt section on page 159 as needed.)

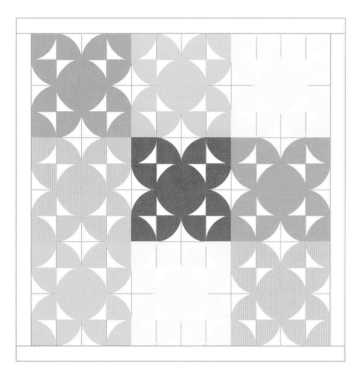

COMPLETED TOP

Ideas for Quilting

- An allover pattern of leaves would be a nice complement to the shape of the blocks as well as the floral theme of the pattern.
- These large blocks create a great canvas to explore individual quilting of block designs. Quilt a flower in the circular centers, and then quilt around the outside of the flower shape with scallops. Then, fill the spaces between the flowers with swirls and feathers.
- If you want something simpler, you could outline stitch around each of the petals.

Answer This:

Take out your quilting journal and ponder these questions.
- What makes an occasion or a life event worthy of a gift quilt? What occasions do you make gift quilts for most often?
- Have you ever made a quilt for charity? If you have, why did you decide to do it? How did you choose the charity you supported?
- If you haven't made a charity quilt, do you plan to? What causes would you like to support with your quilting skills? Why are these causes important to you?

Happiness Practice:
MEANINGFUL FABRICS

Each of us is surrounded with fabrics throughout our lives—and not just those of us who hoard fabric! We wear fabrics, we decorate rooms with them, and we sleep in them. Fabrics don't usually stay with us forever, either; we wear them out, or outgrow them, or otherwise leave them behind. If you love to quilt for the people in your life, then it's your job to swoop in and rescue these meaningful fabrics!

Does your favorite nephew have a pile of T-shirts he's outgrown? These would make a wonderful basis for a quilt he'd treasure. What about your daughter's baby clothes? It may feel uncomfortable to cut them up for quilting, but imagine making a quilt for your first grandchild from that fabric. The curtains, table runner, and aprons from your grandmother's kitchen would piece together into a cheery memento of all the comfort she provided in that room.

Or, if you'd rather not collect meaningful fabrics, you can create them. You can print treasured photographs or children's drawings onto laser-jet fabric. You can also use Spoonflower.com, a service that prints your original designs onto a variety of fabrics in any amount you need (see the Resources section on page 169).

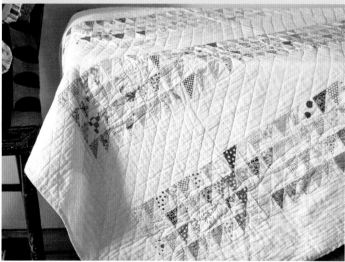

CHAPTER 4

QUILTING TOGETHER

Quilting has a long history as a social craft. You've likely heard about the quilting bees of colonial America, where women would gather to help each other finish quilts. While they were busy sewing, they would share local news and gossip. It was productive time and restful time and community time all rolled into one.

A quilt made by many hands carries special significance, representing a group of people who joined forces as an act of creativity and caring. In this chapter, we'll explore some enjoyable ways to bring your family and friends into quilting. We'll meet a few of the many quilting groups that gather in cities all over the world (not to mention online). We'll also enjoy several quilt projects that are especially nice for making with others.

The SQUARED IN QUILT

FINISHED BLOCK SIZES: 15½" X 15½" (1), 8½" X 8½" (17),
5½" X 5½" (21), 3½" X 3½" (123)
FINISHED QUILT SIZE: 46" X 56"

DIANE: *"The thing I love most about this quilt is it's such a beautiful representation of the word 'community,' with all those interconnected squares."*

CHRISTINA: *"True! And it's also a great quilt to make in quilting-bee fashion, where you divide the work among many hands. The blocks here are based on a very old pattern called Log Cabin, which is made with straight seams, so it's an easy block for quilters of all levels to sew."*

Skill Level:

SUPPLIES

Background: 3¼ yards white solid
Print Squares: 18 fat quarters (or large scraps or quarter yards) in coordinating prints
Backing: 3½ yards your choice of fabric
Binding: ½ yard your choice of fabric
Batting: 49" × 59" (throw/twin size)

FABRICS USED HERE

FreeSpirit Designer Solids: Cream
FreeSpirit: Freshcut by Heather Bailey

CUTTING THE FABRICS

Background/Solid: It's not necessary to cut the selvage off your fabric for this project, but do square the ends of the yardage (see page 151).
Cut 2 strips, 5" × width of fabric
Cut 11 strips, 3¼" × width of fabric
Cut 9 strips, 2¼" × width of fabric
Cut 30 strips, 1½" × width of fabric

Prints (mix and match your prints to the square sizes below):
Cut 1 square, 6½" × 6½"
Cut 17 squares, 3½" × 3½"
Cut 21 squares, 2½" × 2½"
Cut 123 squares, 1½" × 1½"

Christina's Tips

• A design wall comes in very handy for laying out all the blocks of this quilt. If space is an issue, try the Vanishing Design Wall (see the Resources section on page 169), a retractable surface you can install anywhere in your home. Or, try taping the batting for this quilt up on a wall with low-tack painter's tape. You can use this temporary surface to lay out all your quilt blocks, and then when you're ready to assemble the quilt, just take down the batting and use it!

ASSEMBLING THE QUILT BLOCKS

BLOCK A

This one block is made from the 6$\frac{1}{2}$" square and the 5" strips. Use **Diagram A** for orientation.

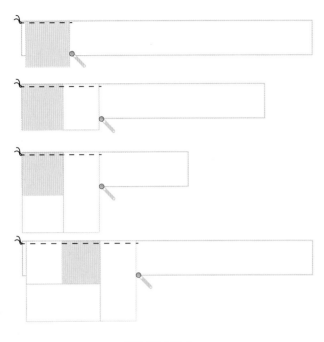

DIAGRAM A

1. Place the 6$\frac{1}{2}$" print square on the 5" background strip, lining up the print square so it's just inside the selvage. Sew the pieces together. Now, place the strip on your cutting surface, line up your ruler with the right edge of the print square, and cut through the background strip. Line up your ruler with the left edge of the print and cut away the background selvage as well. Press the seam allowance toward the print.

2. Sew the finished unit from Step 1 to the 5" background strip. Trim away the excess background strip on the right side and press the seam allowance toward the print square.

3. Sew the finished unit from Step 2 to the 5" background strip. Trim the background fabric to match the right edge and press the seam allowance toward the print.

4. Sew the finished unit from Step 3 to the second 5" background strip. Trim away any excess background on the right and left edges, and press the seam allowance toward the print. Your print square is now encircled in background solid.

5. Square the block to 15$\frac{1}{2}$" × 15$\frac{1}{2}$" (see page 159).

BLOCK B

These 17 blocks are made from the 3$\frac{1}{2}$" squares and 3$\frac{1}{4}$" strips. Use **Diagram B**.

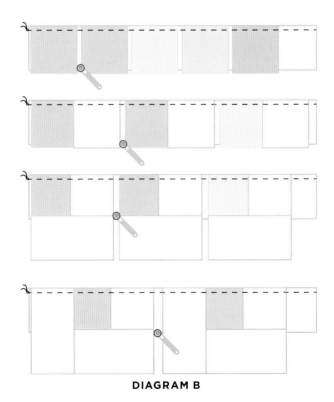

DIAGRAM B

6. Start these blocks with some chain piecing (see page 156). Line up the print squares with the edge of the background strip and sew them one by one. (Try to keep $1/4''$ to $1/2''$ between the print squares.) Lay the strip on your cutting surface and cut the background strip along the right and left edges of each square. Press the seam allowance of each unit toward the print square.

7. Chain piece the finished units from Step 6 to a $3^1/4''$ background strip until it's full, moving to a new strip if you run out of room on the first one. Trim the background strip along the right and left edges of each unit, and then press the seam allowance of each unit toward the print. From this point forward, you don't need to worry about trimming the left edges of these units—you'll take care of that later when you square the quilt blocks.

8. Chain piece the finished units from Step 7 to another $3^1/4''$ background strip, switching to a new strip if you run out of room. Trim the background strip along the right edge of each unit and press the seam allowance of each unit toward the print.

9. Chain piece the finished units from Step 8 to another $3^1/4''$ strip. Trim along the right side of each unit and press the seam allowances toward the print. Square the blocks to $8^1/2'' \times 8^1/2''$ (see page 159).

BLOCK C

10. These 21 blocks are made from the $2^1/2''$ squares and $2^1/4''$ strips. Repeat Steps 6 through 9. Square these blocks to $5^1/2'' \times 5^1/2''$.

BLOCK D

11. These 123 blocks are made from the $1^1/2''$ squares and $1^1/2''$ strips. Repeat Steps 6 through 9. Square these blocks to $3^1/2'' \times 3^1/2''$.

ASSEMBLING THE QUILT TOP

12. Gather the finished blocks into the six groups, consisting of the blocks listed below:

- Group I: 3 Block B, 3 Block C, 24 Block D
- Group II: 3 Block B, 5 Block C, 25 Block D
- Group III: 3 Block B, 3 Block C, 24 Block D
- Group IV: 3 Block B, 5 Block C, 25 Block D
- Group V: 1 Block A, 1 Block B, 1 Block C, 5 Block D
- Group VI: 4 Block B, 4 Block C, 20 Block D

Lay the blocks out, working with one group at a time and following **Diagram C** for placement. You may want to swap a few blocks of the same size between groups so you have an even distribution of prints.

DIAGRAM C

13. Sew the blocks in each group together. Begin by sewing the smallest blocks together, and then begin adding the larger blocks. Try to orient your blocks so that the seams within them are headed in different directions throughout each group. Press the seam allowances to one side or the other as you go, taking care to alternate their directions so you don't have too much bulk at any one point. At the end of this step, you should have six assembled groups.

14. Sew Groups I, II, and III together to form the left side of the quilt top. Press the seam allowances to one side or open. Then, sew Groups IV, V, and VI together to form the right side of the quilt, pressing the seam allowances the same way you did for the left half.

15. Sew the two halves together. Press the seam allowance to one side or open.

BACKING AND FINISHING

Make a 49" × 59" backing. Build a quilt sandwich and quilt. Cut six 2" strips from your binding fabric and bind your quilt. (Refer to the Finishing Your Quilt section on page 159 as needed.)

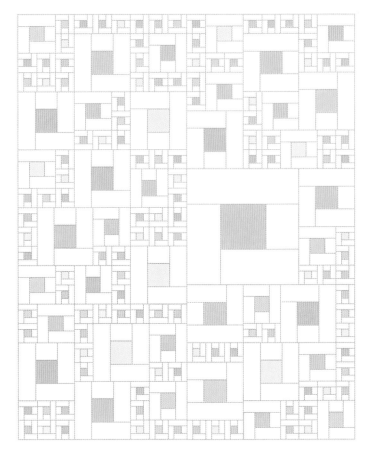

COMPLETED TOP

- -

Ideas for Quilting

- -

- This quilt provides a lovely blank canvas for your quilting imagination! In the sample quilt, you can see a scalloped repeat quilted around each of the larger squares, with swirls wandering between them.
- For a simpler option, stitch an outline around each of the print squares.
- Try stitching with an allover pattern, like stippling or crosshatching.

Tools for Happiness:

WHERE ARE YOUR QUILTING BUDDIES?

If you've reached a point in your quilting life where you're ready to connect with other quilters, here are some good places to begin your search for kindred spirits.

- We recommend starting with all the quilt shops in your local area. These shops often host ongoing quilting circles, and many of them will welcome drop-ins. Or you might be able to take a class and meet some new people there who want to form a group or simply meet for coffee. If your town has fabric stores instead of quilting stores, inquire anyway. If that's where local quilters are getting their fabrics, then maybe the store will consider hosting a regular quilting night.

- You might also check QuiltGuilds.com and TheModernQuiltGuild.com. Both websites offer huge databases of quilting groups meeting in every U.S. state and overseas. (Some guilds, by the way, have annual dues and some don't.) You can also do an online search for "[name of your city and state] Quilt Group."

- Since quilting groups often need plenty of space to meet in (all those sewing machines and big quilts-in-progress), you can also check the bulletin boards of local community centers, churches, libraries, and museums; many of these have rooms that host local quilting groups.

- And if you want to connect with other quilters online, there are groups aplenty, swapping quilt blocks, making the same quilts together, and making quilts for charity. We've listed some of our favorite online groups in the Resources section (page 169), and you can also try an online search for "online quilt groups."

QUILTER STORIES
do.Good Stitches

Rachel Hauser had been quilting for only a few months, but she knew it was becoming a real passion. "I felt very blessed to be able to take up this new hobby and work with such beautiful fabrics," she says, "and I wanted to give something back."

Rachel decided to found a charity quilting circle. She researched both historical quilting bees and modern online quilting groups, and quickly realized that the ideal model for her new group lay somewhere between these two styles. And with that, do.Good Stitches was born.

Rachel saw that "some people have a lot of time to devote to charity quilting and others don't—but they'd like to be involved in a charity effort somehow." So she organized an online circle of ten participants, using the photo-sharing website Flickr.com as a home base. In this circle, five participants took the role of "Stitcher" and five took the role of "Quilter." Each month, one of the Quilters leads the circle, choosing a quilt design and a color scheme. Then each of the ten circle members makes two quilt blocks and mails them to the lead Quilter. The Quilter then assembles, quilts, and binds the project and ships it to the charity. The next month, another Quilter takes over leading and a new quilt begins.

The Stitcher role offers people with time constraints a simple, structured way to participate in charity quilting, and the Quilter role is perfect for people who have more time

to devote. Rachel has a steady waiting list of people eager to sign on as Stitchers, and she adds a new circle each time she finds five new Quilters. By keeping the circles to ten participants, each circle is able to work together easily online, and by keeping the quilts in a modern style, everyone is able to use fabrics from their own stashes to create coordinated quilts.

Within two years, do.Good Stitches has grown into nineteen such circles. Each one supports its own chosen charity, and collectively they produce more than two hundred quilts per year. Rachel says this is the most important thing she's learned from the experience: "Doing even a little bit makes a huge difference. There were so many people out there who have limited time but want to help their communities. We've gotten a lot done by working together."

The TALENT SHOW QUILT

FINISHED BLOCK SIZE: 5½" X 5½"

FINISHED QUILT SIZE: 50" X 60"

CHRISTINA: _"In this project, you can see my obsession with quilt construction in action. Traditionally, this block is made by sewing small squares into the corners of a larger square and then trimming away the excess fabric. It's an easy method, but it creates a lot of waste, so I wanted to find a way to use my fabrics more efficiently."_

DIANE: _"To my mind, the more efficiently you use your fabrics, the more you can splurge on really beautiful ones! This design would be perfect for a quilt block swap. You could ask each participant to use some favorite fabrics in those center squares, or you could send everyone a selection and let them choose."_

Skill Level:

SUPPLIES

Background: 3 yards white solid

Prints: 17 fat eighths in coordinating prints

Backing: 3 yards your choice of fabric

Binding: ½ yard your choice of fabric

Batting: 54" × 64" (twin size)

FABRICS USED HERE

FreeSpirit Designer Solids: Arctic White

Liberty of London Prints: Tana Lawn

CUTTING THE FABRICS

Background:

Cut 18 strips, 5¾" × width of fabric.

Subcut them into 120 squares, each measuring 5¾" × 5¾".

Prints (cut all pieces below from each print):

Cut 2 strips, 4" × 12".

Subcut them into 6 squares, each measuring 4" × 4".

Subcut each of these squares once on the diagonal, creating 12 half square triangles.

Christina's Tips

- The first step of this project is cutting the fabric squares into smaller pieces. You can speed up this process by stacking and cutting a few squares at a time.

- You may notice that, as you're sewing two blocks together, even though you've gotten all the seams to match, the ends of the blocks don't quite line up. If this mismatch is less than ¼", you can correct it by "easing," which is gently stretching the fabric as you sew. Any remaining mismatch will be hidden in the seam allowance. Use a smaller stitch length when you're easing, and steam press the fabric afterward.

ASSEMBLING THE QUILT BLOCKS

1. Place a background square on your work surface **(Diagram A)**. At the top edge of your ruler, locate the 1³/₄″ measurement line. Align it with the top and bottom points of the square. Trim off the right point and discard it. Repeat this step for a total of 40 background squares. These squares are the border squares of the quilt (Block A).

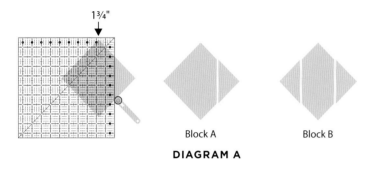

DIAGRAM A

2. For the remaining 80 background squares, repeat Step 1 and then rotate the square 180 degrees. Line it up under your ruler again as in Step 1, and then trim off the opposite point. These units are Block B.

3. Start with Block A, and sew a print triangle to the background piece **(Diagram B)**. The points of the print triangle will extend beyond the background piece a little, so make sure you center them. (See page 154 for more on centering.) Press the seam allowance open. Repeat this process with the rest of the Block A pieces.

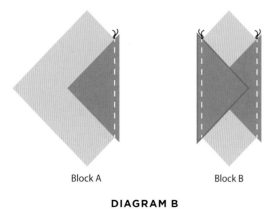

DIAGRAM B

For the Block B pieces, repeat this process again to sew a print triangle to both sides of the background block. These two print triangles should be the same print. Press all the seam allowances open.

4. Square all the blocks to 5¹/₂″ × 5¹/₂″, using this method: start by placing the block on your cutting mat, oriented with a print corner to the top left **(Diagram C)**. Lay your ruler on top, lining it up so that the 5⁵/₈″ measurement lines on the ruler align with the left and bottom edges of the background fabric. (Don't worry about where the ruler lines up on the print triangles; just line it up with the background.) Also, be sure that the ruler's center 45-degree line is running through the diagonal center of the background solid. Trim the right and top edges of the block.

Rotate the block 180 degrees. Lay your ruler over the block again, lining up the 5¹/₂″ marks on the ruler with the left and bottom edges. Double check that the 45-degree line on your ruler is running through the diagonal center of the background solid. Trim the right and top edges of the block. Repeat this process with the rest of the blocks.

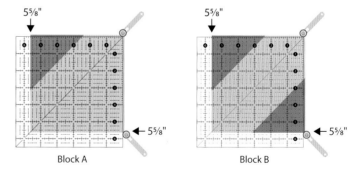

DIAGRAM C

ASSEMBLING THE QUILT TOP

5. Lay out your quilt blocks in 12 rows of 10 blocks each, arranging your prints as you like and referring to **Completed Top** (page 124) for placement.

Or, you might want to try this more mathematical method: Stack your completed A and B blocks, separated by print, and think of the stacks as Print 1 through Print 17. Now, pull the blocks for each row from these stacks, following the number sequence. Your first row consists of Prints 1 through 10, your second row is Prints 11 through 17 plus Prints 1 through 3, and so on.

6. Begin Row 1 by sewing two Block As together. Match the two print corners and pin at both sides of the seam allowance as well as at each end **(Diagram D)**. Press the seam allowance open. Continue sewing Block As together in pairs until you have five pairs, and then sew them together to form Row 1, using **Diagram E** for placement and orientation. Repeat this step one more time to assemble Row 12 of the quilt.

7. Begin Row 2 by sewing a Block A to a Block B **(Diagram D)**. Pin at the seam allowances where the seams meet and at each end. Press the seam allowance open. Repeat this process to sew eight more blocks to this row, making sure the last block is Block A. Refer to **Diagram E** for placement and orientation.

8. Repeat Step 7 to assemble 9 more rows of 10 blocks each. The orientation of the B blocks alternates from row to row; refer to **Completed Top** for placement. Press all seam allowances open.

9. Sew Rows 1 and 2 together, matching all the seams and placing pins in each of the open seam allowances as shown in **Diagram E**. Add Row 3 and Row 4 in the same manner. Press the seam allowance open.

Repeat this process to assemble Rows 5 through 8 into a separate section, and Rows 9 through 12 into a third section. Sew the three sections together, again matching seams as shown in **Completed Top**.

Block A's

Block A & B

DIAGRAM D

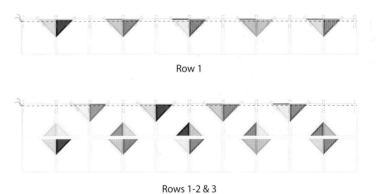

Row 1

Rows 1-2 & 3

DIAGRAM E

BACKING AND FINISHING

Make a 54" × 64" backing. Build a quilt sandwich and quilt. Cut six 2" strips from your binding fabric and bind your quilt. (Refer to the Finishing Your Quilt section on page 159 as needed.)

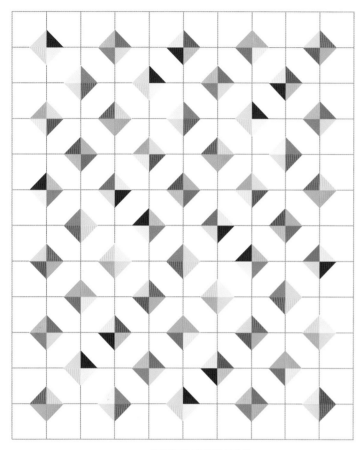

COMPLETED TOP

Ideas for Quilting

- Outline stitch around each of the print diamonds in a zigzag pattern.
- Stitch an allover pattern of loops and swirls to contrast with the sharp angles of the blocks.
- Try hand quilting around each of the print diamonds with a long running stitch, using a complementary floss color.

QUILTER STORIES
Where Have You Found Kindred Quilting Spirits?

"I most often connect with other quilters in the classes I teach at my local quilt shop and in my own studio. I also attend a few local quilt events and interact with other quilters online through Facebook and my website. I'm very friendly with lots of other busy quilt designers and authors, some of whom I may not see for years, but we often stay in touch through e-mail. It's fun to reconnect with them in person at Quilt Market and other national events!"

Meryl Ann Butler, merylannbutler.com

"Most of my initial friendships have come from Flickr.com. It was the place where I met the girl who got me into quilting in the first place some four years ago, and where I met the people I created Fat Quarterly (an online magazine for quilters) with as well. Flickr has been a wonderful place for inspiration, advice, and the support network you would expect from a local guild or group. I've also met amazing people via my blog and other blogs, and my latest obsession is Twitter. The quilty/crafty community on there is unreal. It's like a big old chat room full of like-minded people."

Katy Jones, fatquarterly.com, imagingermonkey.blogspot.co.uk

Creative Exercise:
QUILT-ALONG WITH PRECIOUS FABRICS

Here's a lovely collaborative project for a small group of far-flung (or online) friends or extended family to do together. First, each person should find a piece of fabric that's meaningful to him or her. It might come from a special saved garment, or maybe it's a beautiful vintage find, or it could be some new fabric with a print that perfectly expresses his or her personality. (Some groups also like to establish a specific set of colors for these fabrics, but you don't have to do this.)

Now, each of you will cut your fabric into equal pieces, one for each member of the group. Then you'll all mail or deliver these fabric pieces to everyone else in the group. Each of you will then have an interesting collection of fabrics that represent the whole group, and the basis for making something beautiful and meaningful.

Once everyone has received their fabrics, each of you will use them in a small quilting project of some kind. Your group can agree beforehand to all make the same project, like the Plus You Quilt (page 20) or the Haphazard Chevron

Pillow (page 92). Or maybe each of you wants to choose your own project instead. Set some kind of easy deadline, so that everyone has a finished project to share at the same time.

There are two powerful forms of sharing at work here. First, each of you is sure to treasure this handmade item that represents your whole group. And collectively, your finished projects represent all of your different skills and creative visions. Sharing pictures of them with each other is sure to spark lots of great discussion.

The QUILTER'S TOTE BAG

FINISHED PROJECT SIZE: 15³⁄₄" X 12" X 5"

CHRISTINA: *"I thought it might be fun to include a patchwork project in this book—something with no quilting. Although you could quilt it! I think a bit of hand quilting with a chunky running stitch in the linen around the triangles would be pretty."*

DIANE: *"This tote could make a fun group project for a circle of quilting friends. Everyone could customize her bag with her choice of fabrics. The linen background takes beautifully to customizing."*

Skill Level:

SUPPLIES

Bag Exterior: 1 yard linen, 54" wide (or same yardage for 44/45" quilting cotton)

Bag Accents: ¼ yard (or large scraps) each of 4 coordinating solids

Bag Lining: ½ yard your choice of fabric

Bag Interlining: ½ yard lightweight muslin

FABRICS USED HERE

Robert Kaufman Essex Linen Wide: Flax

FreeSpirit Designer Solids: Manatee, Chamois, Peach Blush, and Celery

Anthology Fabrics: Maya Triangles by Leah Duncan (lining fabric)

CUTTING THE FABRICS

Bag Exterior/Linen:

Cut 1 piece, 17½" × 18¾". (Back of the bag)

Cut 2 pieces, each measuring 3" × 12". (Bag handles)

Cut 1 piece, 5½" × 15½". (Used with Triangle A)

Cut 1 piece, 4¼" × 8½". (Used with Triangle B)

Cut 1 piece, 11" × 20". (Used with Triangle C)

Cut 1 piece, 2½" × 20".

Save the remainder of the linen to cut in Step 12.

Bag Accents/Solids:

From the gray solid, cut 3 pieces: 1 measuring 3" × 3", 1 measuring 3" × 2¼", and 1 measuring 2¾" × 3".

From the peach, chamois, and celery solids, cut 2 strips each, 1½" × width of fabric.

Bag Interior:

Bag Lining: Cut 2 pieces, each measuring 17½" × 18¾".

Muslin Interlining: Cut 2 pieces, each measuring 17½" × 18¾".

Christina's Tips

- For this pattern, you'll need to mark your fabric as you assemble the tote front. We recommend using a FriXion pen, which erases with the heat of your iron (page 149).

ASSEMBLING THE FRONT TOTE PANEL

1. Fold the 3″ × 3″ gray square in half. Place it on your cutting mat and cut from the bottom corner to the top folded corner **(Diagram A)**. This is Triangle A.

    Now fold the 3″ × 2¹/₄″ piece in half so it measures 1¹/₂″ × 2¹/₄″. Repeat the cutting process to create Triangle B. Fold the 2³/₄″ × 3″ piece in half so it measures 1³/₈″ × 3″. Repeat the cutting process again to create Triangle C.

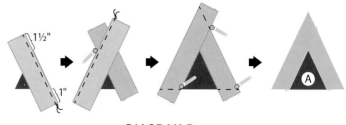

DIAGRAM B

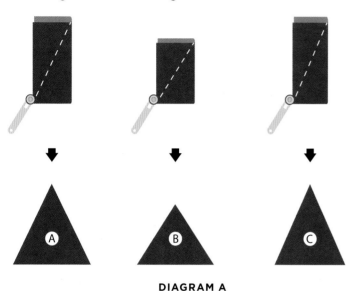

DIAGRAM A

2. Sew a peach strip to the right edge of Triangle A. The end of the peach strip should extend 1″ below the bottom edge of Triangle A (and because it's a long strip, it will of course extend far beyond the top point). After sewing, cut the excess peach strip away, leaving at least 1¹/₂″ beyond the top of Triangle A. Press the seam allowance toward the strip. Now, take the excess strip you just cut away, and sew it to the left side of Triangle A **(Diagram B)**. Again, be sure the end of the strip extends below the bottom edge of the triangle. Trim the excess strip away again, leaving at least 1¹/₂″ beyond the top of Triangle A. (Set the excess aside to use in the other triangles.)

    Before pressing the left-hand strip, use a rotary cutter and ruler to trim the top end of the right-hand strip flush with the seam allowance of the left

strip. Then, press the seam allowance of the left strip toward the strip. Trim the top of the left strip to match the angle of the right strip. Finally, trim the bottom of both peach strips flush with the bottom of Triangle A.

3. Repeat this process to add a chamois strip to the sides of Triangle A. Repeat this process a third time to add a celery strip to Triangle A.

4. Assemble Triangle B and Triangle C in the same manner as Triangle A, placing the colors as shown in **Diagram C**.

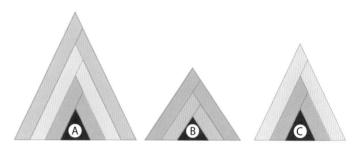

DIAGRAM C

5. Use **Diagram D** for this step. Sew the 5¹/₂″ × 15¹/₂″ linen rectangle to the right edge of Triangle A, matching the centers of the two pieces. (See page 154 for centering.) Press the seam allowance toward the linen. Trim the linen flush with the bottom edge of Triangle A **(see Cut 1, Diagram D)**. Trim the top corner of the linen flush with the left side of Triangle A **(see Cut 2)**. Then, measure along Cut 2, 1¹/₂″ from the top point of the Triangle A.

Mark the linen with an erasable marking tool. (You'll use this mark in Step 8.)

Finally, line the bottom edge of the unit up with a horizontal line on your cutting mat. Measure $2\frac{1}{4}''$ from the right bottom point of the triangle, and trim the linen with a vertical cut **(see Cut 3)**. Discard the excess linen.

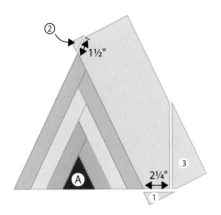

DIAGRAM D

6. Sew the $4\frac{1}{4}'' \times 8\frac{1}{2}''$ linen rectangle to the right edge of Triangle B, matching their centers. Press the seam allowance toward the linen. Trim the linen flush with the bottom edge of Triangle B **(see Cut 1, Diagram E)**. Trim the top end of the linen flush with the left edge of the Triangle B **(see Cut 2)**. Line up the bottom edge of the unit with a horizontal line on your cutting mat, and measure $\frac{1}{4}''$ to the right of the right point of the triangle. Trim the linen with a vertical cut **(see Cut 3, dotted line)**. Discard the excess linen.

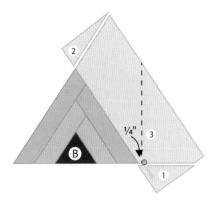

DIAGRAM E

7. Sew the 11″ × 20″ linen rectangle to the right edge of Triangle C, placing the bottom corner of the linen about 1″ below the right point of the triangle **(Diagram F)**. Press the seam allowance toward the linen. Trim the linen flush with the bottom of the triangle **(see Cut 1, Diagram F)**. Line up the bottom edge of the unit with a horizontal line on your cutting mat. Measure about $1\frac{1}{2}''$ to the right of the bottom right point of Triangle C. At about this spot, the edge of the linen should start forming an angle—make your vertical cut here **(see Cut 2)**. Trim the top corner of the linen flush with the left edge of Triangle C **(see Cut 3)**. Discard the excess linen.

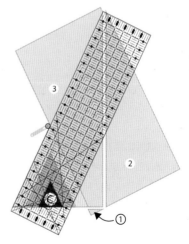

DIAGRAM F

8. Lay the Triangle A unit right side up on your cutting mat, orienting it as shown in **Diagram G**. Lay the Triangle B unit right side up on top of the Triangle A unit, overlapping it just slightly. You'll want the bottom edge of the Triangle B unit to be flush with the bottom edge of the Triangle A unit. Remember that mark you made in Step 5? Line it up with the left edge of the linen on the Triangle B unit. Now, lay your ruler along the left edge of Triangle B and trim. Discard the excess linen from the Triangle A unit.

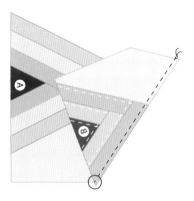

DIAGRAM H

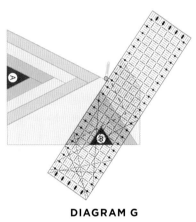

DIAGRAM G

9. Orient these two units as shown in **Diagram H** and sew them together. The bottom left point of Triangle B should extend 1/4″ below the linen, so that the bottom edges of both pieces will align after sewing. Press the seam allowance toward the linen.

Place the piece on your cutting board and lay your ruler along the top edge of Triangle A **(Diagram I)**. Trim the linen of Triangle B flush with Triangle A.

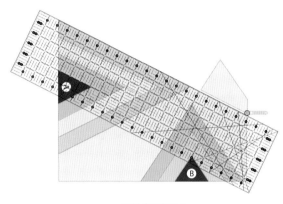

DIAGRAM I

10. Sew the 2 1/2″ × 20″ linen strip to the Triangle A-B piece along the edge you trimmed in Step 9. Press the seam allowance toward the linen strip. Now, trim the right end of the strip flush with the right side of the piece **(see Cut 1, Diagram J)**. Sew the Triangle C unit to the strip, orienting it so the point of the triangle extends 1/4″ beyond the edge of the strip. Press the seam allowance toward the linen strip.

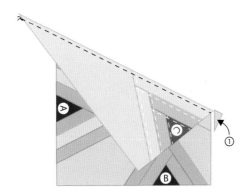

DIAGRAM J

11. Trim the excess fabric from the left edge to form a rectangular block **(Diagram K)**. Square this block along the other three edges as needed (see page 159). Your finished piece should be approximately 12″ × 15½″. Don't worry if it's not exactly this size; you can make adjustments in the next step.

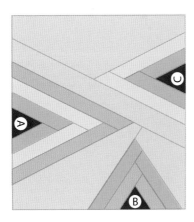

DIAGRAM K

12. Cut the rest of the linen, customizing its measurements to fit the actual size of your finished block. If your block measures 12″ wide, cut 2 strips, each measuring 3½″ × 15½″. If your block is less than 12″ wide, you'll need to cut these strips a little wider. Here's how to figure out how much wider: take the number of inches your block is short in width, and divide that amount by two. Then, add that number to the width of your two fabric strips.

So, for example, if your block is 1″ short in width, you'll add ½″ to the width of each strip, making them 4″ × 15½″.

Sew these linen strips to the Triangle A and Triangle C edges of the block **(Diagram L)**, pressing the seam allowances toward the strips. Trim the panel to 17½″ wide, making sure you trim the same amount from both sides—you want your block to be centered. Trim any excess linen from the top and bottom edges of the strips.

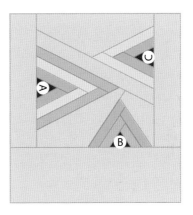

DIAGRAM L

13. If your block is 15½″ high, cut one 4½″ × 17½″ strip of linen. (Again, if your block less than 15½″ high, add more to the width of this strip.) Sew this strip to the Triangle B edge of your block and press the seam allowance toward the strip. Trim the panel to 18¾″ tall. The finished panel should measure 17½″ × 18¾″.

ASSEMBLING THE TOTE HANDLES

14. Fold one of the 3″ × 12″ linen strips in half lengthwise, right sides facing, and sew along the long raw edge. Press the seam allowance open and turn the handle right side out. Press it flat, orienting the seam in the center of one side. (The seam side is now the wrong side of the handle.) Edge stitch ⅛″ from both long edges. Repeat this step with the other linen strip.

15. Lay one handle flat with the wrong side facing up. Measure 2″ in from each end and place pins at these spots. Fold the handle in half again lengthwise, wrong sides together, stopping at the pins. Reposition the pins so they hold the fold together at these points **(Diagram M)**. Edge stitch through both layers of the handle from the first pin to the second, backstitching at the beginning and end of the seam. Repeat this process with the other handle.

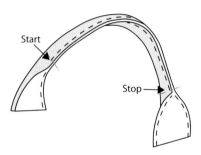

Start

Stop

DIAGRAM M

ASSEMBLING THE TOTE

16. Cut a 2¹/₂″ × 2¹/₂″ square from each of the bottom corners of the front bag panel **(Diagram N)**. Repeat this process to cut the back bag panel in the same manner.

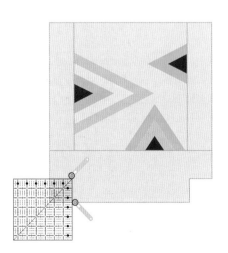

DIAGRAM N

17. Pin the front panel to the back panel with right sides facing. Sew along the right, bottom, and left edges—don't sew where the corners are cut away **(Diagram O)**. Press the seam allowances open.

DIAGRAM O

18. Pull the front and back panels away from each other. Match and pin the seams at the center of one open corner **(Diagram P)**. Sew along the raw edge and press the seam allowance open. Repeat this process with the other corner.

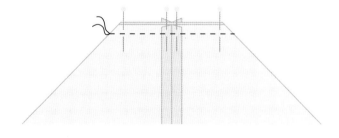

DIAGRAM P

19. Repeat Steps 16 through 18 two more times: once using the muslin interlining and again using the bag lining. When you work with the bag lining, leave an opening of about 6″ in the center of one of the side seams; you'll use this later to turn the bag right side out.

20. Turn the exterior of the bag right side out. Find the center points of the front and back panels and place pins to mark them. Pin one handle to each side of the bag, right sides facing and matching the raw edges of the handle with the top edge of the bag. Each end of the handle should be about 4″ from the center of the bag panel.

21. Slip the muslin interlining into the exterior of the bag. Match and pin the side seams of the two layers. Pin the layers in a few more locations around the top edge of the bag. Slip the whole bag into the lining, right sides facing. Again, match and pin the side seams and place more pins around the top edge to hold the three layers together. Sew around the top edge of the bag with 1/4″ seam allowance, backstitching over the handles to secure them.

22. Turn the bag right side out through the opening in the side seam of the lining. Sew this opening closed, either with a ladder stitch (see page 155), or by machine using a scant 1/16″ edge stitch. Push the lining and muslin layers into the bag.

23. Press the top edge of the bag, flattening the seam. Edge stitch 1/8″ from the top edge of the bag.

Answer This:

Take out your quilting journal and ponder these questions.

- What happens when you quilt with other people? Does the act of making affect the conversations you have?
- Do you feel more comfortable quilting with just a few people, or in a larger group?
- Have you ever tried to teach someone to quilt? What was that experience like? If you had it to do over, how might you approach this teaching differently?
- What ideas in this book resonated with you? What have you learned about yourself?

Laid Back Ladies of the Block

In 1985, Teresa Haskins invited a small group of friends to her home in Lynwood, Washington, to quilt. They all belonged to a local quilting guild with hundreds of members, and wanted a more intimate group experience, where they could really get to know each other. That group, which came to be known as "Laid Back Ladies of the Block," is still meeting twice a month more than twenty years later.

These twelve women have supported each other through quilt show deadlines, graduations, marriages, divorces, illnesses, deaths, and, more recently, the births of several grandchildren. As member Carol Porter says, "Quilting has brought us such a deep connection; these women are like family, and somehow even more than family." Member Betty Howland adds, "Being part of this group, you always have someone you can count on."

In the group's earlier years, they would often collaborate on quilts, sharing in making the blocks. But more recently, the group has settled into a rhythm of less quilting and more enjoying each other's company. They take retreats together twice a year, where, as member Carol Henry puts it, they "eat, quilt, eat, chat, eat, stay up late, eat, sew, eat, piece, baste, knit, and eat." And they still collaborate on the occasional quilt—usually, to celebrate the birth of a member's first grandchild.

When asked what's given their group such longevity, these women grow thoughtful and offer a few ideas. The size of the group is a definite factor, they feel. With no more than twelve members, they've always been able to meet in someone's home, where there's space and time to truly connect. They've also been careful to steward the mix of personalities. They use the term "gentle souls" to describe how no one in the group tries to dominate or dictate. If a member leaves the group, they select a new member very carefully, inviting her to a few meetings to see if the fit is right.

"We've made an effort over the years to keep our group in harmony," Carol Porter says, "but at the same time, that harmony feels effortless to us."

What about the future? As Carol Porter shares, "We are noticing, now that we're twenty years older, that quite a few of us are starting to have health issues. We make light of it, because it's so prevalent now. We have an intuitive sense of sisterhood and acceptance that we'll always be together, to the end. Our numbers will dwindle over time, but some of our daughters are coming into the group. We have a sense that our bond will continue through our daughters and their friends."

Creative Exercise:

MAKE A NEW QUILTER

"Will you teach me how to quilt?" Once you've been quilting for a while, your friends may begin popping this question. And while it's definitely rewarding to help someone you love discover a whole new passion, we quilters know that our craft can require a certain amount of patience and meticulousness.

So perhaps the best way to figure out how to introduce a friend to quilting is to spend a little time looking at how they approach nonquilting tasks like planning and problem solving. These traits will give you some important keys to how you might best approach teaching them to quilt.

For example, let's say your new student loves planning ahead, keeps a detailed calendar, and is always on time. They're a good candidate for patchwork! You can show them how to plan where each fabric color will be in the quilt design, and how to cut and organize the pieces. You can walk them through the steps of assembling the quilt block, showing them how each seam leads to the next. All of this will appeal nicely to their methodical mindset.

On the other hand, if your freewheeling, live-in-the-moment friend wants to learn to quilt, you might want to start with a very small project, like a set of coasters. One coaster might be strip pieced, another made from whole cloth, and yet another made from half square triangles. That way, your student can stay

engaged in the ever-changing process, while still learning basic quilting skills. Or, if you want to make an entire quilt together, maybe improvisational piecing is the way to go: your student can sew pieces of fabric together with no pattern.

Similarly, you might know someone who likes to solve problems by diving right in and trying out solutions. It might make sense to start them with a design of simple squares. Their forge-ahead personality might not want to linger in the planning and piecing of a complex pattern.

But what if you have a student who prefers to solve problems by carefully thinking through all of their options? For their first quilt project, try a simple two-color pattern, just to keep the number of creative decisions to be made at a minimum. Then you'll be able to give better focus to the process of piecing and assembling the quilt.

If you aren't sure how to tell what your student's planning and problem-solving styles are, try taking a peek at whatever kind of day planner or calendar they use. Is it meticulous? Haphazard? Filled with notes and lists? Filled with doodles? That should give you some ideas. Or, if you can, observe them at their job. We're very often in planning and problem-solving modes in our workplaces.

The ODDS and ENDS QUILT

FINISHED BLOCK SIZE: 15½" X 15½"

FINISHED QUILT SIZE: 57" X 75"

DIANE: *"That's intricate piecing—like quilts within a quilt! This seems like another of those meditative designs, where you can take your time and focus deeply on the process."*

CHRISTINA: *"It definitely is. And, perhaps oddly, this is one of my favorite kinds of quilts to teach. Many newer quilters shy away from a detailed block like this, but I love seeing how empowered they feel once we've broken it down into smaller pieces. There's nothing like witnessing that moment when a student gets all those seams to match perfectly. It's so exciting."*

Skill Level:

PIECED BY HEATHER LOTT

SUPPLIES

Background: 1¾ yards gold solid

Light Prints: ¼ yard each of four prints

Dark Prints: ½ yard each of four prints

Sashing/Borders: 2 yards gray solid

Backing: 3½ yards your choice of fabric

Binding: ½ yard your choice of fabric

Batting: 61" × 79" (twin size)

FABRICS USED HERE

Cloud 9 Fabrics: Miscellany by Julia Rothman

FreeSpirit Designer Solids: Manatee

Kona Cotton Solids: Curry

CUTTING THE FABRICS

Background/Gold Solid:

Cut 4 strips, 5¾" × width of fabric. Subcut them into 24 squares, each measuring 5¾" × 5¾".

Cut 24 strips, 1½" × width of fabric. Do not subcut them.

Light Prints (cut all pieces below from each print):

Cut 1 strip, 5¾" × width of fabric. Subcut it into 6 squares, each measuring 5¾" × 5¾".

Cut 1 strip, 1½" × width of fabric. Do not subcut it.

Dark Prints (cut all pieces below from each print):

Cut 1 strip, 3½" × width of fabric. Subcut it into 12 squares, each measuring 3½" × 3½".

Cut 5 strips, 1½" × width of fabric. Do not subcut them.

Sashing/Gray Solid:

See page 154 for more on cutting sashing and border strips.

Cut 2 strips, 3½" × 72" from *length* of fabric. Subcut these into 8 lengths, each measuring 3½" × 15½". (Block sashings)

Cut 2 strips, 3½" × 69½" from *length* of fabric. (Side borders)

Cut 2 strips, 3½" × 57½" from *length* of fabric. (Top and bottom borders)

Cut 3 strips, 3½" × 51½" from *length* of fabric. (Row sashings)

Christina's Tips

- Look for solids that won't overpower your prints, so there's a nice balance of positive and negative in your quilt.

ASSEMBLING THE QUILT BLOCKS

You'll assemble three base units individually, and then sew them together with a cut square to make the final block.

HALF SQUARE TRIANGLE UNIT

We'll refer to Half Square Triangles as HSTs. See page 155 for details on making them.

1. Begin with the $5^3/4'' \times 5^3/4''$ squares of background solid and prints. Pair one print square with one background square and assemble four HSTs. Press the seam allowances toward the print. Repeat this process with the rest of the $5^3/4'' \times 5^3/4''$ squares.

2. Square each of these HSTs to $3^1/2'' \times 3^1/2''$. You should have 24 HSTs from each of your four prints, making a total of 96 HSTs.

PRINT STRIP UNIT

3. Sew a $1^1/2'' \times$ width of fabric strip of background solid to each side of a same-size strip of one of your light prints **(Diagram A)**. Press the seam allowances toward the print.

4. Square the left edge of the unit, then subcut it into 12 pieces, each measuring $1^1/2'' \times 3^1/2''$. Repeat this process with the remaining light print strips, creat-

ing a total of 12 print strip units per print, or 48 total.

NINE-PATCH UNIT

5. Use **Diagram B** for Steps 5 through 8. Sew a $1^1/2'' \times$ width of fabric dark print strip to each side of a same-size strip of background solid. Press the seam allowances toward the print. (This is Strip Set A.) Repeat this process to make a second Strip Set A of the same print. Repeat this process again with the rest of the dark prints, creating a total of eight Strip Set As.

6. Sew a $1^1/2'' \times$ width of fabric strip of background solid to each side of a same-size strip of one of your dark prints. Press the seam allowances toward the print. Repeat this process with all four dark prints, creating a total of four Strip Set Bs.

7. Square the left edge of each strip set, and then subcut it into 27 pieces, each measuring $1^1/2'' \times 3^1/2''$. You should now have 54 Strip Set A pieces for each print (216 total) and 27 strip set B pieces for each print (108 total).

8. Sew a Strip Set A piece to each side of a Strip Set B piece (all three pieces should be the same print). Press the seam allowances away from Strip

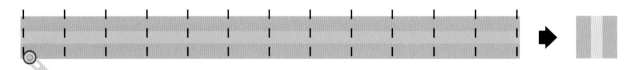

DIAGRAM A

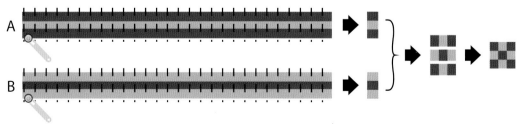

DIAGRAM B

Set B. Repeat this process with all of the strip set pieces to create a total of 27 units per dark print (108 total).

FINAL BLOCKS

It's a good idea to separate your finished units by type and print, and designate your light and dark fabrics as in **Diagram C**: D1 through D4 for your dark prints, and L1 through L4 for your light prints.

In **Diagram C**, you'll notice that there are four variations of the final block. It's helpful to sew all three blocks of each variation at one time, so you don't accidentally mix up your fabrics. Keep your finished blocks sorted into stacks by variation.

Ⓐ	Ⓑ	Ⓒ	Ⓓ
D3	D4	D1	D2
L4	L3	L2	L1
L2	L1	L4	L3
D1	D2	D3	D4

DIAGRAM C

9. Sew the units for each row together, using **Diagram D** for placement and orientation. Follow the pressing directions below:

- Row 1: Press the seam allowances toward the HSTs.
- Row 2: Press the seam allowances away from the nine-patch units.
- Row 3: Press the seam allowances toward the print strips.
- Row 4: Press the seam allowances away from the nine-patch units.
- Row 5: Press the seam allowances toward the HSTs.

10. Sew Rows 1 through 5 together in order, following **Diagram D**. Nestle all the seams together where they meet (see page 157). Press the seam allowances toward Rows 1, 3, and 5. Your final block should measure 15$\frac{1}{2}$" × 15$\frac{1}{2}$".

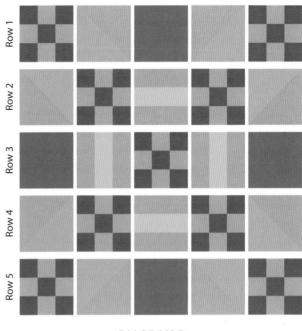

DIAGRAM D

ASSEMBLING THE QUILT TOP

At this point, you can set all the previous letter designations aside and label your stacks of finished blocks as A, B, C, and D, referring back to **Diagram C**.

11. To assemble Row 1, sew a Block A to a 3$\frac{1}{2}$" × 15$\frac{1}{2}$" sashing strip **(Diagram E)**. Sew a Block B, another sashing strip, and a Block C to the row. Press all seam allowances toward the sashing strips.

12. Assemble Row 2 in the same manner, using Block D, Block A, Block B, and two sashing strips. Press all seam allowances toward the sashing strips.

13. Assemble Row 3 using Block C, Block D, and Block A with sashing strips in between. Press all seam allowances toward the sashing strips.

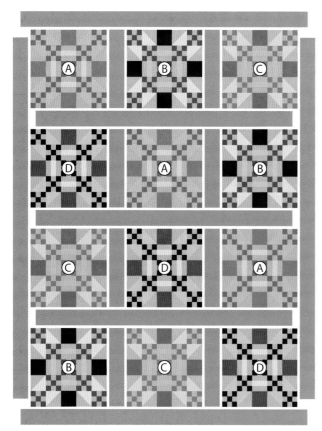

DIAGRAM E

COMPLETED TOP

14. Assemble Row 4 using Block B, Block C, and Block D with sashing strips in between. Press all seam allowances toward the sashing strips.

15. Sew Rows 1 through 4 together, with a 3¹/₂″ × 51¹/₂″ sashing strip between the rows. Press the seam allowances toward the row sashing strips.

16. Sew the 3¹/₂″ × 69¹/₂″ side border strips to the right and left edges of the quilt. Press the seam allowance toward the border strips. Sew the 3¹/₂″ × 57¹/₂″ border strips to the top and bottom of the quilt and press the seam allowances toward the border strips.

BACKING AND FINISHING

Make a 61″ × 79″ backing. Build a quilt sandwich and quilt. Cut seven 2″ strips from your binding fabric and bind your quilt. (Refer to the Finishing Your Quilt section on page 159 as needed.)

Ideas for Quilting

- The sample quilt is quilted with a fun loopy pattern, reminiscent of wishbones from a turkey. It's a simple pattern with a traditional feel that complements the traditional look of the quilt.
- For a different look, try crosshatching within each of the blocks, following the diagonal lines in each of the base blocks. Then, quilt something fun and loopy within the sashings and borders for contrast—or try a longer variation of the crosshatching.
- If you like tie quilting, try a tie in the center of each of the nine-patch units.

Creative Exercise:
QUILTING WITH FAMILY

We all know that a quilt can be a splendid heirloom gift, commemorating a special event like a wedding, graduation, first home, or new baby. If you're making a special quilt for someone in your extended family, why not make it a true family affair and involve your spouse and children in the making?

Don't panic! There are plenty of easy ways you can bring nonquilters, both young and old, into the process of creating a quilt. At the end of the journey, every member of the family will have contributed meaningfully to the finished product, and this makes the gift all the more special. Consider these ideas:

- You may not want younger children handling pins or scissors, but they can help choose the fabrics for the project. (If you want to steer clear of superheroes and purple dinosaurs, just present your helper with a few pre-screened options.) If your kids are old enough to tie knots, consider tie quilting your project; this method gives the whole family plenty of helping to do.

- Older kids might enjoy acting as advisers when you're choosing a quilt pattern. You might also be able to convince them to sit down at the sewing machine and piece a simple backing, or if not, they can press your seams, which might help the piecing process move along more quickly.

- Your spouse can be a great second pair of hands for assembling the quilt sandwich (which is another good project for older kids, too).

Or you might just design your quilt in a style that lets each member of the family contribute to it visually. You can always give young kids some squares of fabric and fabric markers, let them go to town drawing, and then sew the resulting works of art into your quilt. Older kids might like to try their hands at simple appliqué with fusible webbing. Your spouse might like to try some block printing with fabric paints.

And of course, you can purchase fabric sheets that will run through your ink-jet printer, and simply print fabric photos of each member of the family to stitch into the quilt. Each member could embellish his or her own photo in some way for an extra creative touch. Be sure to let everyone sign his or her name to the quilt in some way, too.

The POINTS of INTEREST QUILT

FINISHED BLOCK SIZE: 10½" X 10½"

FINISHED QUILT SIZE: 50" X 60"

CHRISTINA: *"When I made this design, I was playing with modern interpretations of quilts using the Drunkard's Path block. Not a week later, I saw an antique quilt in this same pattern. I did a little digging and discovered that it was first referred to as the 'Snowball Quilt' back in 1934."*

DIANE: *"It's kind of fun how, no matter how modern quilting gets, it's always tied somehow to its traditional roots."*

Skill Level:

SUPPLIES

Background: 3¼ yards white solid

Prints: ⅜ yard each of 15 coordinating prints

Backing: 3 yards your choice of fabric

Binding: ½ yard your choice of fabric

Batting: 54" × 64" (twin size)

Templates A and B (located on page 173)

FABRICS USED HERE

FreeSpirit Designer Solids: Arctic White

FreeSpirit: Flea Market Fancy by Denyse Schmidt

CUTTING THE FABRICS

Background/White Solid: Cut 10 strips, 11½" × width of fabric. Subcut them into 30 squares, each measuring 11½" × 11½".

Prints: Cut 2 squares, each measuring 11¼" × 11¼" from each print.

Christina's Tips

- You'll find a 10½" (or larger) square ruler handy for squaring your blocks.

ASSEMBLING THE QUILT BLOCKS

1. Fold a background square into quarters with wrong sides facing, aligning all the raw edges. Lightly press the folds. Place Template A onto this square, lining up the straight edges of the template with the raw edges of the fabric. Cut around the curve of the template through all four layers with a rotary cutter **(Diagram A)**. Repeat this process with the remaining background squares to create a total of 120 Template A pieces.

2. Fold a print square into quarters with wrong sides facing, aligning all the raw edges. Press the folds. Place Template B onto this square, lining up the straight edges of the template with the *folded* edges of the fabric **(Diagram A)**. Cut around the ends and curve of the template through all four layers with a rotary cutter. Repeat this process with the remaining print squares to create a total of 30 Template B pieces.

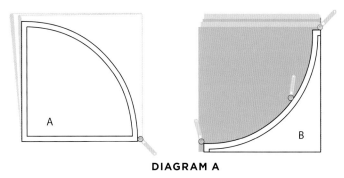

DIAGRAM A

3. Pin one Template A piece to one Template B piece **(Diagram B)**. (See page 156 for more on working with curves.) Sew around the curve and press the seam allowance toward the background fabric.

Repeat this process to attach three more Template A pieces to the remaining curves of this Template B piece. To save time, finger press each seam allowance toward the background, and then press the whole block with an iron.

4. Repeat Step 3 with the remaining Template A and B pieces to create 30 completed blocks.

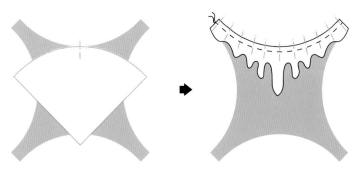

DIAGRAM B

5. Square these blocks to 10½" x 10½", using this method: place a block on your cutting surface, orienting it as shown in **Diagram C**. Lay your ruler over the top, aligning its 5¼" measurement lines with the centers of each of the four points at the block's edges. Trim the top and right edges of the block. Rotate the block 180 degrees and repeat this process.

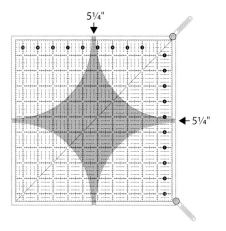

DIAGRAM C

ASSEMBLING THE QUILT TOP

6. Divide your blocks into two groups of 15 blocks; each group should contain one of each of your 15 print fabrics. You'll make Rows 1 through 3 from the first group of blocks, and Rows 4 through 6 from the second group. Lay your blocks out in an arrangement you like, referring to **Diagram E**.

7. Sew the first two blocks of Row 1 together. Match the seams at each of the print points and pin the seam allowances together securely **(Diagram D)**. Press the seam allowance open. Repeat this process to add the remaining three blocks to this row. Repeat this process again to assemble the five remaining rows.

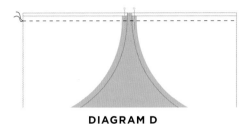

DIAGRAM D

8. Sew Rows 1 and 2 together, matching the seams at the points. Press the seam allowance open. Repeat this process to add Row 3.

9. Assemble Rows 4 through 6 into a separate section in the same manner. Sew the two sections together, pressing the seam allowance open.

BACKING AND FINISHING

Make a 54" × 64" backing. Build a quilt sandwich and quilt. Cut six 2" strips from your binding fabric and bind your quilt. (Refer to the Finishing Your Quilt section on page 159 as needed.)

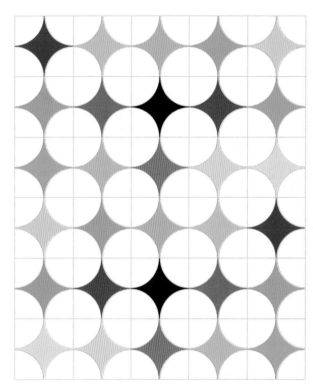

DIAGRAM E

Ideas for Quilting

- Quilt a simple outline stitch around the inside edge of the print shapes. Then, outline stitch around the circles in the background.
- If you're feeling adventurous, quilt feathered wreaths in each of the open circles and then outline stitch around the prints.
- This is a great quilt top for tie quilting. Place a tie in each of the centers of your prints and in the centers of the background circles.

CHAPTER 5

TOOLS *and* TECHNIQUES

Over time, every quilter collects an assortment of favorite tools and some preferred ways to approach the common tasks of quilting. In this chapter, we'll share our favorites, and offer some general tips that might be useful as you make the projects in this book. We'll also give you detailed instructions for finishing your quilts.

TOOLS FOR QUILTING

If we had to choose an essential tool kit for quilting, we'd include these items (see the Resources section on page 169 for more information).

Rotary Cutters (a, b; see page 148): It's helpful to have both a 45mm and 28mm rotary cutter on hand. The 45mm **(a)** is great for larger cuts, like cutting long strips from yardage or squaring large blocks or quilts. We use a 28mm **(b)** cutter most of the time, for smaller cuts, curved cuts, and squaring.

Self-Healing Cutting Mat: If you have the space and budget for a 24" × 36" mat, buy one—you won't regret it!

Rulers: Quilting rulers are available in a seemingly endless range of shapes and sizes. We think a 6" × 24" ruler is essential; it comes in handy for many tasks, including cutting strips from yardage and squaring quilts before binding. (We'll talk about some other favorite sizes later on.)

Pins: For quilting, we like long, glass-head (or pearl-head) pins and long, flat flower-head pins. (Both types are often sold under the name "quilting pins.") The glass-head pins are perfect for general piecing—you can iron right over the heads and they won't melt. Flat flower-head pins are best for squaring quilts. Because they're flat, you can lay a ruler on top of them without losing accuracy.

Scissors (c, d, e; see page 148): A general pair of sewing scissors with an 8" blade **(c)** is great for cutting large pieces of batting or fabric. A pair of appliqué scissors **(d)** will help you cut batting out of seam allowances in smaller projects like bags. They're also useful for clipping into a seam allowance. A pair of 5" knife-edge scissors **(e)** is handy for snipping away threads or bits of fabric when you're piecing.

Seam Ripper (f): A seam ripper has a pointed tip for slipping under stitches, and a tiny curved blade for cutting them. Replace your seam ripper regularly! A dull one can make removing stitching more difficult and can even damage fabrics.

Iron and Ironing Board: Look for an iron that can produce high temperatures and steam, and has an automatic shutoff and a long cord. Look for an ironing board with a large ironing surface, plenty of padding, and adjustable height.

Hand Sewing Needles: For hand quilting, look for quilting needles (also called "betweens"). These come in a range of sizes, and they're all rather short but very sharp, so you can easily glide them in and

out of a quilt. It's also a good idea to keep some size 8 or 9 embroidery needles on hand; they're useful for hand sewing the edge of a binding.

Sewing Machine Needles: It's wise to keep a supply of sewing machine needles on hand. Needles slowly dull over time, and you can usually feel this happening: when you begin to feel more resistance as the needle glides through your fabric, it's time to change needles. Always install a fresh needle at the start of a new quilt project.

For the projects in this book, you'll want to choose a needle size between 75/11 and 90/14. (The smaller the number is, the better the needle will work with finer weight threads.) Look for "sharps" or "quilting" needles, but the "universal" ones will also

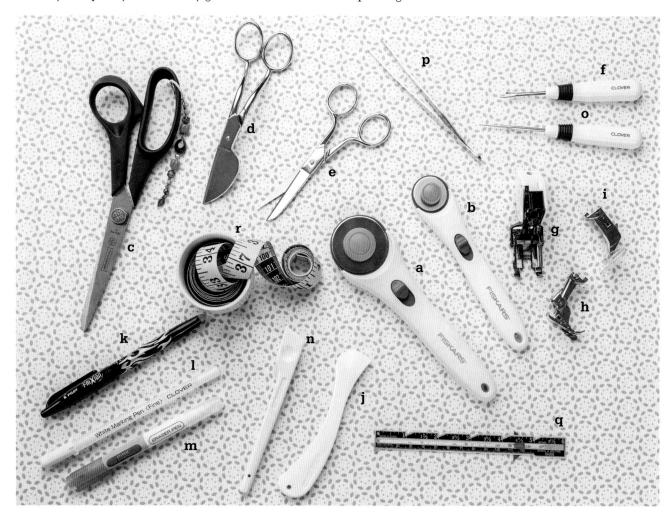

work just fine. Choose one that's appropriate for the fabric and thread you're using in your project.

Once you have the essential tools for quilting, you might want to pick up some of these useful specialty tools. See the Resources section on page 169 for more information.

Walking Foot (g): This presser foot makes quilting much easier, and it's also useful for sewing binding to a quilt. When you feed several layers of fabric and batting through a walking foot, it guides them all with even pressure, so the layers won't shift. Check with the dealer for your sewing machine to find out which model is right for you.

Patchwork Foot (h): This type of presser foot usually has a prominent fabric guide that helps keep fabric aligned for a ¼" seam. You can sew a ¼" seam with your regular presser foot, of course, but you may find it easier and more accurate with a patchwork foot. Again, check with your sewing machine dealer.

Curve Master Presser Foot (i): Designed to fit any sewing machine model, this presser foot produces curved seams with no pinning.

Hera Marking Tool (j): This tool makes crease marks on fabric to guide your stitching or cutting.

FriXion Pen (k): This pen wasn't originally designed as a quilting tool, but it's been embraced by quilters because it makes marks on fabric that you can easily remove with the heat of an iron. If you need the marks to return, place the fabric in your freezer for a few minutes and they magically reappear!

White Marking Pen (l): If you're working with dark-colored fabrics, this pen makes marks that turn white as they air-dry. Just moisten or iron the marks to remove them.

Chacopen Erasable Pen (m): Lines from this pen will erase with exposure to air within 2 to 10 days, or you can use the attached eraser.

Finger Pressing Tool (n): This tool quickly flattens and lightly creases seam allowances, saving wear and tear on your fingers.

Sewer's Awl (o): You can poke this tool through two or more layers of fabric to keep them together as you're feeding them through your sewing machine.

Tweezers (p): Tweezers are great for pulling loose threads or feeding fidgety fabric pieces under the presser foot for those last few stitches.

Seam Gauge (q): This small ruler has a sliding plastic marker, so you can set a particular measurement and then easily check it against your fabric as you move it around your project. It's especially useful for checking seam allowances.

Measuring Tape (r): Sometimes you need to do quick measurements in very long lengths, like on a roll of batting or bolt of fabric. A flexible measuring tape provides a portable option.

Additional Rulers: In addition to the essentials we mentioned earlier, here are some sizes that come in handy: 3" × 18", 15" square, 10½" square, 6" square, 4" square, and 3" square. Look for rulers that have measurement lines in ⅛" increments as well as angle lines.

For the long rulers you use day to day, you might also want to invest in safety shields, which are long strips of clear plastic that attach to the ruler, protecting your fingers from the rotary cutter blade. They also make it easier to lift and reposition your rulers.

MATERIALS FOR QUILTING

Here's a general overview of the materials you'll need for the projects in this book.

TYPES OF FABRIC

Quilter's Cotton: This type of fabric has a firm enough structure that it's easy to sew and press, while still being light and breathable enough to keep a finished quilt comfortable. It also needs no special care, which means you can toss your quilts in the washer and dryer for years. These days, you can even find organic cotton fabrics, which are produced with materials and methods that have less impact on the environment. You'll find some of our favorite organic manufacturers in the Resources section.

Voile: We think this soft, sheer cotton fabric deserves a larger role in quilting. Clothing made from voile can stand up to repeated washing and wear, so it will perform just as well in a quilt. And a voile quilt feels so lovely to the touch!

Linen: We think linen also deserves a larger role in quilting! It can take a lot of abuse, and it gets softer with repeated use. Yes, linen wrinkles, but that natural crinkle only adds to the visual and textural appeal of a quilt.

Clothing: When you make a quilt from a loved one's clothing, you can get a hug whenever you need it. If the garments have been stored for a while, give them a good wash with a detergent like Biz or OxiClean, which are gentle on vintage pieces and older stains. Let the clothes soak in your washing machine for a bit before starting the wash cycle. When they're clean and dry, cut them apart at their seams to create flat pieces you can cut up for quilts.

THREAD

All the projects in this book were made with Aurifil 50/2 cotton thread. It works well for all stages of a project—piecing, quilting, and binding. Either cotton or polyester thread will make a nice quilt, so feel free to experiment and choose for yourself.

BATTING

All the projects in this book were made with Warm and White Cotton Batting, a mid-loft batting from the Warm Company. There are many different kinds of natural and synthetic battings on the market, and you can absolutely choose your favorite mid-loft brand for these projects. No matter which kind of batting you choose, keep in mind that there's always a certain potential for shrinkage and shifting. A cotton batting with a small percentage of synthetic fiber in it, or an all-cotton batting that has been needle-punched, will help to prevent both of these issues. (Look at the packaging for the minimum recommended distance between quilting lines, and follow that to minimize shifting as well.)

If you're working with white or light-colored fabrics, look for a batting that's been whitened, because natural-colored cotton batting often contains darker flecks that can show through.

PREPARING FABRICS FOR QUILTING

Proper fabric preparation will start you down the path to a beautiful, long-lasting quilt.

Prewashing: There are some good arguments for prewashing fabric; it removes chemicals from the manufacturing process and it eliminates shrinkage. Even so, we prefer to work with unwashed fabrics most of the time. Many fabrics are easier to work with when they're fresh off the bolt, because prewashing always leaves cottons a little wrinkly. (You can minimize wrinkles by ironing the fabric while it's still slightly damp.)

That said, if you're making a quilt with lots of saturated colors, prewashing is wise! And if you make a quilt with saturated colors and forget to prewash, try adding ½ cup of salt and ½ cup of white vinegar to a cold-water wash, and then soaking your quilt for a half hour before you start the wash cycle. Most of the time, this technique helps keep the colors from bleeding.

Prewashing will cause your fabric to fray a bit at the ends. You can minimize this by pinking the edges of the fabric with pinking shears or a rotary pinking blade. Be warned, though: even with pinked edges, prewashed fabric will still do some fraying. If you're a fan of prewashing, add a little extra to the yardages in this book to compensate.

Squaring Yardage: Before you start cutting your yardage into pieces, square the end. It only takes a few minutes, and it makes cutting and piecing your quilt so much easier.

Begin by pressing your yardage with a hot steam iron, removing the crease at the fold. Then, take the fabric in your hands and fold it in half with the right side out, lining up the two selvage edges. You'll probably find that when you also try to match up the cut edges, the fold will be puckered. Start sliding those selvage edges from side to side until the fold becomes flat and smooth again. (Now, the cut edges will likely be out of alignment.) Place the yardage on your ironing board and lightly press a crease at the new fold.

Next, place the folded fabric on your cutting mat with the fold closest to you. Lay a long ruler over the fabric, aligning it very close to the left edge but in a position where you can still cut through both layers **(Photo A)**. Take a second ruler (an 8½" × 12" one works well), and line it up against the right edge of the first ruler. Line up a ½" measurement line at the bottom of the right-hand ruler with the folded edge of the fabric—and as you're doing this, keep the two rulers lined up right next to each other **(Photo B)**. With this alignment, you're ready to square.

Move the right-hand ruler out of your way, being careful not to disturb the left one **(Photo C)**. Cut along the right edge of the ruler with a rotary cutter. You've now squared the left edge of your fabric **(Photo D)**, so this will be the edge to work from when you make the cuts specified for your project.

QUILT-MAKING TECHNIQUES

This section will cover the techniques you'll need to make the projects in this book, but it's by no means a comprehensive guide to quilting. There are so many wonderful books for the beginning quilter; check the Resources section on page 169 for some we recommend.

CUTTING TECHNIQUES

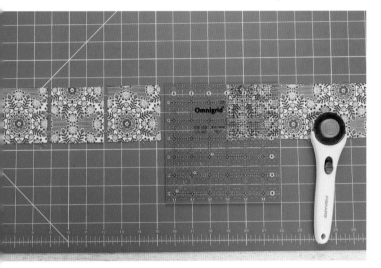

Subcutting Fabric Strips: For most of the projects in this book, you'll begin by cutting the fabric into large strips, and then subcutting these into smaller pieces. In some cases, you'll sew several strips together lengthwise, and then subcut that unit into smaller pieces. When you're subcutting, two details are important: first, always begin measuring and cutting from a squared edge of fabric; and second, keep a close eye on the bottom edge of your ruler as you're making subcuts. You'll want to keep a clear measurement line on your ruler lined up with the bottom edge of the fabric, so all of your subcuts are square. Take a moment to realign your ruler before you make each new cut. If you notice that your ruler has wandered into a slight angle, just take a moment to resquare the edge of the fabric before you make any more subcuts.

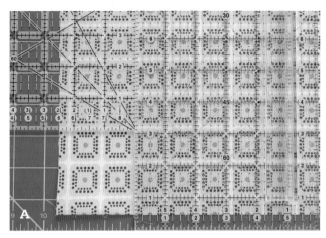

Cutting When Your Ruler Is Too Small: Sometimes, a project will require you to cut strips that are wider than any of the rulers in your collection. You can save yourself a purchase by simply placing two rulers side by side **(Photo A)**. For example, if your ruler is 6" wide but you need to make an 8½" cut, you can place one ruler at the left edge of your fabric, aligning its 2½" measurement line with the squared edge of the fabric. Then place a 6"-wide ruler right next to it, and use that one as your cutting ruler. Slide the left-hand ruler along the left edge of the fabric before you make the cut, and adjust the position of the other ruler as needed to be sure you are making a square cut.

When you need to cut a strip of yardage that's longer than your ruler, you can measure the length of the cut you need to make, and then make a small snip into the fold of the fabric at that point with your scissors. Then, lay the fabric flat on your cutting mat and smooth out any wrinkles. Place your ruler on the fabric at the snip you just made, lifting the right edge of it a little so you can make sure your ruler is lined up precisely on the left edge of the cut **(Photo B)**. Then, align a ½" line at the bottom of the ruler with the fold, and make the cut.

Cutting Sashing and Border Strips: For some quilts, you'll need to cut very long strips of fabric for borders or sashings. Use the technique above to cut your yardage to the length specified in your project. Then, lay the fabric on your cutting mat with its fold closest to you. Fold it in half crosswise, lining up the selvages along the top edge. Fold it in half crosswise again, still keeping those selvages lined up. Go ahead and fold it one more time if necessary, until the fabric will fit under the length of your ruler. (We like a 24" ruler for this process; it keeps you from having to cut through too many layers of fabric at once.)

Reposition the folded fabric on your cutting mat, placing the selvage edge to the left. Align your long ruler at the selvage edge of the fabric, and use a second ruler to help you establish a square edge. Trim away the selvage. Now, use this squared edge to line up your ruler and start cutting your strips.

BASIC SEWING TECHNIQUES

Here are a few helpful techniques you can use in any quilting project.

Sewing Accurate ¼" Seams: Although your sewing machine's base plate has a ¼" seam allowance mark, it's still a good idea to check whether your machine's ¼" seam is accurate. Sew a ¼" seam on a piece of scrap fabric and then measure the seam allowance with a ruler. If the seam allowance is more or less than ¼", don't worry—you can make a new mark on your base plate. Take a piece of scrap paper, and draw a line exactly ¼" from one of its straight edges. Position this paper under your sewing machine needle, placing the straight edge to your right. Lower the needle into the paper right on the line you drew. Then, mark where the edge of the paper is on the base plate, using tape or a permanent marker. This mark is your new guide to an accurate ¼" seam.

Adjusting Sewing Tension: If you can see bobbin thread showing at the top of your seams, your machine's tension is too tight and needs loosening. If you can see the top thread showing at the underside of your seams, your machine's tension is too loose and needs to be tightened. Check your manual for instructions on how to make adjustments.

Pressing vs. Ironing: In most quilt projects, you'll need to press your seams, but not iron them. What's the difference? When you're ironing, you're generally moving your iron over the fabric, which in turn pulls the fabric around. Pressing means setting your iron on top of the fabric and pressing it straight down.

If you iron a seam allowance, you often end up with an uneven seam—and sometimes, with your stitches peeking out between the pieces of fabric. If you press that seam, you'll have a neat line where the two pieces meet.

Finger Pressing: This technique is exactly what it sounds like: instead of using an iron, you'd lightly crease the fabric by pressing it with your fingers.

Finding Centers: In several projects in this book, we'll direct you to find the center of a piece of fabric before pinning or sewing it. The simplest way to do this is to fold the fabric in half, carefully matching all the edges, and finger press a little crease to mark the center. You might want to place a pin at this crease before flattening the fabric out again.

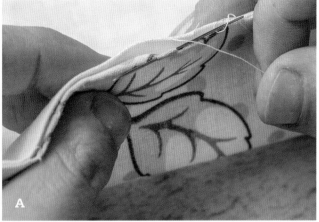

PIECING TECHNIQUES

Here are the piecing techniques you'll need to make the projects in this book.

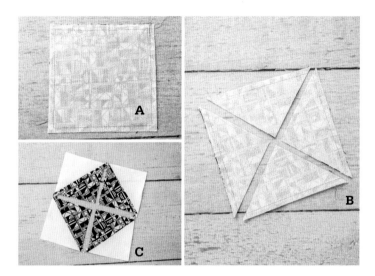

Sewing a Ladder Stitch: This invisible hand stitch is useful to close an opening in a seam. We'll assume that the opening in your fabric has two folded edges, and you might find it helpful to pin them together. Begin by inserting your needle between the folds, and bring it back out through the seam just outside the end of the opening. (This allows you to hide the knot in your thread inside the opening.) Now, insert your needle into one of the folds, and take about a $^1/8$" stitch through the edge of the fold. Bring the needle out, and then take a $^1/8$" stitch through the edge of the opposite fold **(Photo A)**. Pull the thread through and then repeat this process, stitching into one fold and then the other. When you reach the other end of the opening, tug the thread taut to close the opening **(Photo B)**. Knot the thread and bury the end in the fabric.

Making Half Square Triangles: You can use this method (devised by Jenny Doan of Missouri Star Quilt Company) with any size of fabric square. Check each project for specific dimensions.

1. Pair up two fabric squares with right sides facing. Sew them together along all four sides with a ¼" seam allowance **(Photo A)**. Don't leave any openings in this seam.

2. Cut this square into quarters along both diagonals **(Photo B)**. It's okay to cut through your stitching from the previous step.

3. Open these four squares and press their seam allowances **(Photo C)**.

4. Finally, square your half square triangles to the size specified in your project. Place a ruler over the square, lining up its diagonal measurement line with the diagonal line of the half square triangle. Trim the top and right edges so the piece is slightly larger than the final measurement you need. Rotate the piece 180 degrees, realign the ruler as before, and trim the top and right edges to the final measurement.

How to Calculate the Size of a Half Square Triangle

If you want to incorporate some half square triangles into a project, and you know what finished size you need them to be, here's a simple method for figuring out what size fabric squares you'll need to start with.

Take the width measurement you want for your finished half square triangle. Divide this number by 0.6, and round the result up to the nearest quarter inch. So, for example, let's say you need half square triangles that measure 2¼". That 2¼" divided by 0.6 equals 3¾", so you'd need to use 3¾" fabric squares to make these half square triangles. Once you have the measurement you need, it's a good idea to make a test half square triangle and verify that the pieces end up being the correct size. And if you want to give yourself a little extra insurance, you can always add an extra ¼" to your squares and trim them to size when you square the finished half square triangles.

Chain Piecing with Strips: When piecing a quilt involves sewing lots of same-size pieces to lots of other same-size pieces, this method saves time. Instead of cutting all of the individual pieces you need from both fabrics, cut them from only one fabric, and leave the other as a long strip. Then, sew the cut pieces of fabric along this strip one after the other, keeping them ¼" to ½" apart **(Photo A)**. When you're finished sewing, cut the strip with a ruler and rotary cutter to separate the sewn-on pieces.

Chain Piecing with Blocks: If your project involves making many copies of the same pieced unit, you can use a slightly different form of chain piecing. Sew the first pair of pieces together—and don't remove it from your sewing machine or cut the thread. Keep

sewing for a few more stitches, even though you aren't sewing on any fabric. Then feed in two more pieces of fabric and sew them together **(Photo B)**. Repeat this process, taking a few stitches between units, and you'll end up with a long thread with all your pieced units on it. Just clip them apart and press them.

Working with Curved Seams: Some quilters fear curved seams, and that's too bad—curves open up all kinds of beautiful design possibilities. When you're working with curved pieces of fabric for the projects in this book, one of them will be a convex (or outward) curve, and the other will be a concave (or inward) curve. They can be tricky to pin together, so the best way to begin is to locate their centers. We do this by carefully folding each curved edge in half.

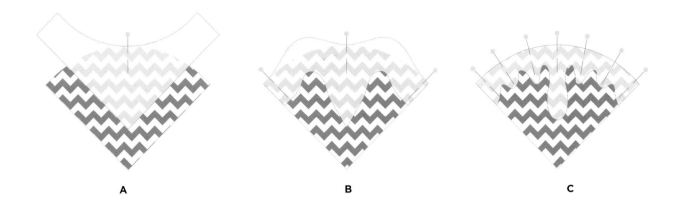

A   B   C

Fold a convex curve by matching up the corners at either end of the curve. Smooth the curve flat and give the fabric a good finger press at the fold. The crease you make is the center of the curve; place a pin to mark it. If you're working with a concave curve, start the fold by matching the straight edges at the ends of the curve. Then smooth the fabric, finger press the fold, and place a pin at the crease to mark the center.

Pin these two pieces together at their center points **(Diagram A)**. Then, match up the end points of the two edges and pin them again, so you now have a total of three pins **(Diagram B)**. Finally, begin pinning the edges together between these pins, keeping the fabric smooth and even between pins **(Diagram C)**. It's a good idea to use a lot of pins when you pin a curved seam; the fabrics need to stretch just a little so they lie flat against each other, and plenty of pins will prevent that stretch from creating puckers in the seam. When you sew the seam, you can carefully sew over these pins (if you're comfortable doing that) or remove them as you sew.

Matching and Nestling Seams: You'll often encounter points in patchwork where two seams meet up. You'll want these seams to match precisely, and all this usually requires is a little attention to pressing and pinning.

Throughout this book, you'll notice that we give very specific instructions as to which directions to press your seam allowances. We do this so that, when you do have two seams that need to match, their seam allowances will usually be pressed in opposite directions. This helps the two seam allowances nestle together, which in turn helps keep the seams matched up as you sew. Before you pin the pieces together, carefully fold the top layer back and make sure the seams match **(Photo A)**. We also recommend placing a pin through each of the seam allowances to help keep everything aligned as you sew.

In some cases, you'll need to match two seams that have their seam allowances pressed in the same direction. Pair these seams up with right sides facing, and pinch them together with your fingers an inch or so from the raw edge of the fabric. Then, peel back the layers to make sure the seams are aligning **(Photo B)**. Keep pinching the fabric together, place a pin at both sides of the seam, and then release your hold.

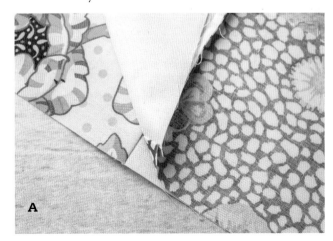

A

B

When you need to match seams where the seam allowances have been pressed open, you can double-check the alignment by gently pulling the two sides of the seam away from each other. The key here is to loosen only the top one or two stitches **(Photo C)**. This tiny opening, which is well within your seam allowance, helps you make a perfect match. Pin both sides of the seam allowance to keep the pieces aligned while you sew.

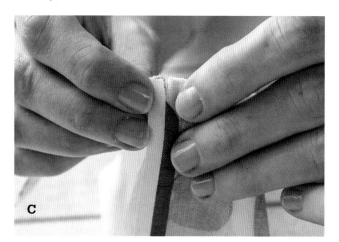

C

Clipping into a Seam Allowance: In a piece of complex patchwork, you may have several seams coming together. Sometimes we alleviate bulk in these spots by clipping into one of the seam allowances. Clips are usually done at the center of a seam **(Photo A)**. Be careful to clip only up to the stitching, but not through it! Once you've clipped into the seam allowance, press the two halves of the seam allowance in opposite directions **(Photo B)**.

A

B

SQUARING QUILT BLOCKS OR PIECES

We square for two reasons: to make sure the sides of a block are even with one another and at perfect 90 degree angles; and to make sure the patchwork is centered within the block.

Every quilter needs to square, because every process of quilting—cutting, sewing, pressing—can create tiny variations. Squaring is just a simple way to correct your block so it's ready for the next step of your quilt.

In several of the projects in this book, we've given you precise, step-by-step instructions for squaring. But in other cases, we've simply instructed you to

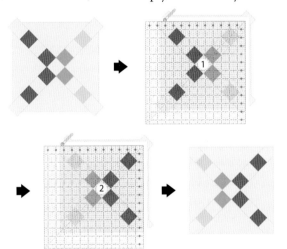

"square the block." Here's a general squaring process for these instances.

First, there's a little math involved in squaring. Measure the current width of the block. Then, find the block size specified in your project instructions. What's the difference between these two numbers? Divide this difference in half. The result is the amount you'll need to trim from both sides of the block.

Place the block on your cutting surface and lay a ruler over it. Line up a clear measurement line at the left and bottom edges of the ruler with the left and bottom edges of the block. Trim the block along the top and right edges. Then, rotate the block 180 degrees and place the ruler over it again. Once again, line up clear measurement lines at the left and bottom of the ruler with the left and bottom of the block, and trim the top and right edges.

If this all seems too complicated, don't overthink it. All you really need to do is cut the edges of your block so they're square, the design is centered, and they're the right size. You can absolutely do this by eyeballing in many cases. In the project instructions throughout this book, we'll tell you what size your blocks should be after squaring.

FINISHING YOUR QUILT

In this section, we'll cover the three steps that are common to every quilt project: backing, quilting, and binding.

ASSEMBLING THE BACKING

Assembling a Simple Backing: All of the quilt projects in this book specify yardage for making a single-seam pieced backing. Simply cut your backing yardage in half along its width. Then cut one of the selvages off of each piece. Pin the two pieces together

with right sides facing along the edge where you cut away the selvage. Sew them together and press the seam allowance open or to the side.

A finished backing should be 2" larger on all four sides than its quilt top. If your backing is larger than this, you can trim it down to the correct size.

Assembling a Pieced Backing: You may wish to be a little more creative, piecing your backing from several fabrics. Pieced backings are nearly as easy to make as single-seam backings: simply grab some large pieces of fabric and begin sewing them together until you reach the backing size your project requires. In **Diagram A**, you can see some examples of how you might approach this piecing. Pieced backs offer a great opportunity to use up large scraps. If you have an extra block or two left over from a quilt project, it's fun to incorporate these into a pieced backing.

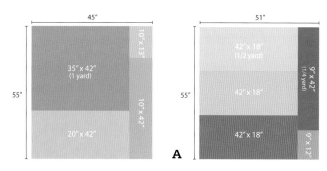

A

As you're piecing a backing, the only thing you need to pay some attention to is the number of seams. If your pieced backing contains a lot of seams, the added bulk can become a bit cumbersome when you're quilting the quilt. You may prefer to press the seam allowances of your pieced backings open to keep bulk down.

PREPARING A QUILT SANDWICH

To begin, find a surface large enough to lay your quilt flat. If you don't have access to a large table, an expanse of floor works as well. It's always a good idea to sweep or vacuum the floor before you lay your quilt pieces down. (Incidentally, if you find that you don't have a space big enough to lay out your quilt, try talking with your local quilt or fabric shop. Many have classroom space where you can lay out a quilt sandwich.)

Lay your backing out first, with the right side facing down. Carefully tape the edges of the backing to your work surface with low-tack painter's tape,

stretching the fabric so it's smooth and taut but not tight enough to stretch the seams. Lay the batting on top of the backing, centering it as best you can. Smooth out any wrinkles and bumps until the batting is nice and flat. Finally, lay the quilt top, right side up, on top of the batting, centering it as best as you can. Smooth out any wrinkles and bumps. If you like, you can also use an iron to help smooth everything out, but if you do, make very sure the surface you're using won't be damaged by the heat.

BASTING YOUR QUILT

We're fans of basting with a needle and thread. It's simple to do, it keeps the layers of your quilt securely together, and you can easily quilt over it in any pattern. But some quilters place safety pins all over the sandwich to hold the layers together. Some prefer to use basting spray, which is a light spray adhesive that sticks fabric and batting together. If you want to explore either of these methods, try an online search for more details.

The basting stitch is simply a series of long running stitches. (See what it looks like on page 162.) Begin basting at the center of your quilt sandwich, stitching across the quilt both vertically and horizontally. Then baste across the quilt on both diagonals. After that, continue basting in vertical and horizontal rows, working from the center out to the edges. Depending on the size of your project, place these rows of basting 2" to 6" apart.

Incidentally, if you're making one of the smaller projects in this book, such as the Liberty Mini Quilt Art, the Haphazard Chevron Pillow, or the Pocket Wall Caddy, you might want to baste with somewhat smaller stitches, so you can fit more of them on the project and keep its layers more stable.

When you have the layers of your quilt basted together, you're ready to start quilting.

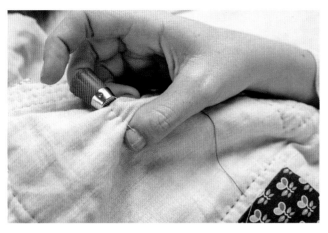

QUILTING YOUR QUILT

You can absolutely quilt any small project in this book on a domestic sewing machine using a walking presser foot. But we don't think it's all that easy, unfortunately, to quilt a full-size quilt on a domestic machine. It's challenging to maneuver your quilt around while you're trying to stitch even a simple pattern, and the weight of the quilt as it hangs from the machine can put stress on the piecing seams.

To be fair, however, we should also mention that there are quilters who do amazing, detailed quilting using domestic machines. This technique is often called free-motion quilting, and it's a subject outside the scope of this book. In the Resources section on page 169, we've listed two excellent books on the subject. In this section, we'll focus instead on two easy options for any quilter: hand quilting and hiring a professional longarm quilter.

Quilting by Hand: A hand quilted quilt has a warm, inviting look, and you can hand quilt without much special equipment. The downside of hand quilting, of course, is that it takes a lot of time. It's definitely a meditative process, and if you're willing to slow down and enjoy the moment, it could even become one of your favorite parts of quilting.

Tools for Hand Quilting (see page 161): You'll find supplier information in the Resources section.

- **Thimbles (a):** The traditional metal thimble is certainly functional, but there are newer variations on the market that might be more comfortable and easier to use. Clover's Protect and Grip Thimble, for example, has a metal tip for pushing your needle and soft, elastic rubber sides that help you grip the needle.

- **Needle Threader (b):** Quilting needles have a very small eye, which helps them glide more easily in and out of your quilt. It also makes them trickier to thread, so a needle threader is a big help.

- **Needle Grabber (c):** This flat rubber disk helps you grip and pull needles through thick fabrics or multiple layers. Needle grabbers are especially useful when you're tie quilting (a method we'll discuss later in this section).

- **Binder Clips (d):** These clips, which are specially designed for fabric, are useful for holding sections of your quilt in position, and also for applying binding.

- **Marking Tools (e, f):** We talked about Hera markers **(e)** and erasable fabric pens **(f)** in the Tools for Quilting section (page 147). For hand quilting, you'd use these markers to draw your quilting design on the quilt before you stitch it. You can draw freehand or use a ruler to draw straight lines.

- **Needles (g):** Quilting needles come in a range of sizes, and the smaller the needle you use, the smaller the quilting stitch you can achieve. If you're new to hand quilting, make a little test sandwich with some scraps of fabric and batting, and try out several different needle sizes and stitch lengths. See what feels most comfortable to you.

Quilting Without a Frame

Some quilters prefer to use a quilting frame for hand quilting, but we don't think it's necessary. As long as your quilt is well basted, we think you'll find it easier to maneuver it around in your lap unframed. And incidentally, working with a quilt in your lap, and scrunching it this way and that, makes it very soft by the time you're finished quilting.

- **Embroidery Scissors (h):** Since the only cutting you need to do in hand quilting is snipping threads, a small pair of embroidery scissors is perfect. Two styles are shown in the photo.

- **Quilting thread (i):** It's a good idea to use a thread specifically manufactured for hand quilting. These threads are of heavier weight and made from three strands, so they stand up to the uneven tension your hands create as you're quilting. You can use embroidery floss in place of quilting thread if you want a more prominent stitching line.

Stitches for Hand Quilting: All of these stitches are extremely easy to do, and they offer slightly different looks on your finished quilt.

- **Running Stitch/Basting Stitch (A, top three rows):** This is a versatile stitch—you can vary the length of your stitches and the spaces between them to match the look of your quilt. (And if you make the stitches long enough, as in the top row, they become basting stitches.) The running stitch is generally more noticeable and decorative than the quilting stitch. To start a running stitch, insert your needle down through the quilt layers, and then pull the knot so it pops through the fabric and nestles into the batting. Bring the

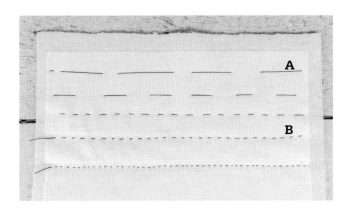

needle back up again, then back down, then back up. (Essentially, your needle is making a rocking motion, and this technique gives you more even stitching.) Pull your thread through, and then continue on in this manner.

- **Quilting Stitch (B, bottom two rows):** The quilting stitch is very similar to the running stitch, but you're taking much smaller "bites" of fabric with each stitch. To begin a quilting stitch, push your needle into the fabric, pulling the knot to hide it inside the batting. As soon as the needle penetrates the backing fabric, rock it back up through the layers. Pull your needle through the fabric to create a small stitch, and then push it right back down into the fabric. Continue this rocking motion for four or five stitches before pulling the needle and thread through again.

- **Tie Quilting:** If you'd like to do much less stitching, consider tie quilting—it's a perfect complement to many quilt tops. You can tie quilt with a variety of materials, including pearl cotton, embroidery floss, yarn, or cotton crochet thread. Choose a needle that's appropriate to your yarn or thread but has a sharp point.

  The simplest method for tie quilting is to insert your needle into the quilt top from front to back, going through all the layers, and then coming back up through the layers about ¼" away. Clip the thread, leaving a 2" tail on both sides of the stitch. Then, tie these strands together in a double knot. To make this process go faster, you can make a lot of these stitches at one time. Don't clip your thread between them; just leave long stitches of thread on the surface of your quilt. Then, when you reach the end of the strand, clip the thread between these stitches and knot the ends.

  The downside of tie quilting is simply that, no matter what material you use for tying, its ends will tend to fray and mat over time. Keep in mind, too, that ties can catch and snag, placing stress on your quilt. If you're making a quilt that will see lots of heavy use, it's usually wiser to quilt it by machine or with a quilting stitch.

Working with a Longarm Quilter: If you'd rather not hand quilt, you can always hire a professional quilter with a longarm sewing machine to do it for you. Longarm quilting can be significantly faster and neater than what most of us can accomplish at home, and it's often surprisingly affordable. The other benefit of longarm quilting is that it gives you much more freedom to quilt beautiful patterns in your quilts. Most of the projects in this book were quilted on a longarm machine.

If you decide to hire a longarm quilter, you'll need to prepare your quilt sandwich according to his or her specifications. You'll usually find detailed preparation instructions on a longarm quilter's website.

SQUARING YOUR QUILT

Instead of squaring their quilts, some quilters cut away the excess backing and batting so they are flush with the edges of the quilt top. This is a perfectly acceptable way to prepare a quilt for binding, but it's possible that the edges of your quilt won't quite match up when you fold it. If you prefer a squared quilt, here are two methods for creating one.

Squaring a Quilt Without Borders:

1. Fold your quilt in half in any direction. Lay it on your cutting mat so you can access one end. Grab some flat-head quilting pins.

2. Insert a pin into an easily identifiable point a few inches from the edge of the quilt (a point where several seams match is good). Push this pin through the layers to the other side of the quilt. You're aiming to have this pin pass through the same spot in the piecing on the opposite side of the quilt **(Photo A).** Reposition the pin and shift the quilt until you have that alignment. Then, carefully secure the pin through the layers to hold them in place (without shifting the quilt). Repeat this process a few more times in different spots along the edge of the quilt, keeping the pins a few inches from the edge.

3. Use a large ruler, preferably 6" × 24". Line it up along the edge of the quilt and position the ½" measurement line on the ruler along the fold. (Push down firmly on the ruler to make sure it's positioned as accurately as possible.) If it helps you align more easily, you can place a second ruler on its edge at the fold of the quilt with one hand, and with your other hand move the primary ruler so it butts up to that second ruler **(Photo B).**

4. Now, make sure your ruler is not only aligned with the fold of the quilt, but close enough to the edge that you'll be trimming away only a scant portion. If the edge of your quilt is longer than your ruler, begin cutting at the fold, and when you run out of ruler, slide the quilt toward you. Reposition the ruler, line it up with your previous cut, and continue trimming the edge.

5. Finally, flip your quilt over so you can access the opposite edge. Repeat Steps 1 through 4 at this edge. Then, refold the quilt in the other direction and repeat Steps 1 through 4 for both of these edges as well.

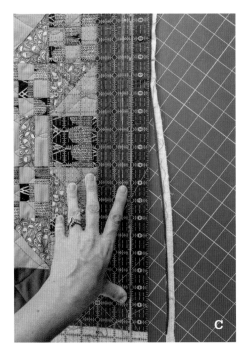

Squaring a Quilt with Borders: When your quilt has border strips on all four sides, the squaring process becomes a bit simpler. Use the seam where the border was sewn to the body of the quilt as a cutting guideline. Just choose a measurement line on your ruler to align with this seam, and then trim through all the layers along the edge of the quilt **(Photo C)**. As with a borderless quilt, you want to trim as little as possible from the quilt edges. And of course, you'll want to trim those edges so that all the borders are the same width.

BINDING YOUR QUILT

For the quilts in this book, we've used a double-fold binding. This method involves some hand stitching, but we think it's easier on the whole than installing a binding with machine sewing.

Assembling a Binding Strip

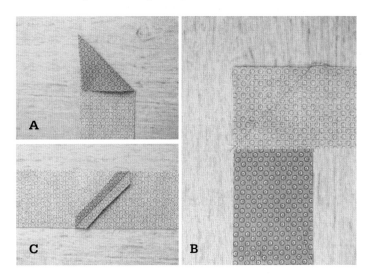

1. Begin by cutting strips on the straight of the grain from your binding fabric, 2" × width of fabric. Your project instructions will tell you how many strips you'll need.

2. Take one of these strips, and fold one end on the diagonal with wrong sides facing **(Photo A)**. Repeat this process with all but one of the binding strips, folding them in the same direction each time.

3. Take the remaining strip that you didn't fold and lay it flat with the right side facing up. Take one of the strips with the folded end, open up the fold, and place this strip over the first one at a right angle **(Photo B)**.

4. Place a pin at each end of the crease and then sew along the crease.

5. Trim the seam allowance to ¼" and press the seam open **(Photo C)**. Repeat this process to add the rest of the binding strips until you have one continuous strip.

6. Press the finished strip in half along its length with wrong sides together, making sure the raw edges match. You are now ready to sew it to your quilt.

Sewing the Binding to the Quilt

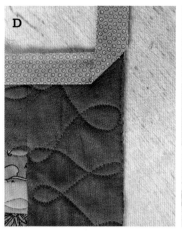

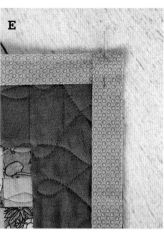

1. Start at about the center of one edge of the quilt. Pin the end of the binding strip to the quilt, lining up the raw edges. Leave a tail of about 12" of binding unsewn at this starting point; you'll use it later.

2. Begin sewing the binding strip to the quilt with a ¼" seam allowance, keeping the raw edges aligned as you sew. When you're ¼" from the first corner, stop sewing and backstitch to secure the seam. Clip your thread.

3. Fold the binding strip straight up, so it's perpendicular to the edge of the quilt and it creates a diagonal fold (Photo D). Then fold the binding back down again, keeping the diagonal fold in place as you do (Photo E). You'll create another fold in the binding as you do this,

and that fold should be flush with the raw edge of the quilt. Pin the binding to hold it at the corner, and then begin sewing the binding to the next edge of the quilt. Backstitch at the beginning of this section, and again ¼" before the next corner.

4. Continue sewing the binding to the quilt along all four sides in this manner. When you reach a point about 12" from where you started sewing, stop and backstitch to secure the seam. Clip this end of your binding to about 6" long; it should extend about halfway into the gap in the binding seam.

5. Lay a ruler on top of this end of binding, lining up the edge of the ruler with the edge of the binding (Photo F).

6. Now, lay the other loose end of the binding along the edge of the quilt and over the top of the ruler. Fold this end back on itself, placing this fold about 2" above the bottom of the ruler (Photo G). (This measurement gives us just enough fabric to join the ends of the binding neatly.) Cut through the fold and discard the excess binding strip.

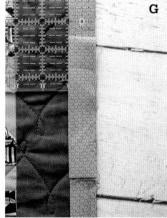

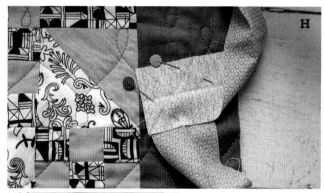

7. Now, take the two loose ends of the binding strip and unfold them. Fold the end of one strip on the diagonal and press a crease. Then, pin the strips together at a right angle **(Photo H)**. You may need to scrunch up the quilt a little so you can get the strips into the right position.

8. Sew the binding along the diagonal crease and trim away the excess fabric, creating a ¼" seam allowance **(Photo I)**. Press the seam allowance open and then fold the binding in half lengthwise once again. Now it should fit the quilt perfectly! Sew the remaining binding strip to the edge of the quilt.

9. Press the binding away from the quilt now. Flip the quilt over so you're facing its back, and thread a needle for stitching the binding down by hand.

10. Sew the edge of the binding to the back of the quilt with a blind stitch **(Photo J)**.

How to Blind Stitch

1. Starting just outside the stitch line where you sewed the binding to the quilt, push your needle down through the backing fabric and batting and then back up through the layers about ½" away. Pull your thread taut, being sure to bury your knot in the batting of the quilt.

2. Now, fold the binding over the edge of the quilt so it just barely covers the point where your thread is exiting the backing. This positioning is what makes a blind stitch invisible to the eye.

3. Insert your needle into the fold of the binding, directly above the spot where the thread is exiting the quilt. Make sure your needle is passing inside the binding, between its layers of fabric.

4. Leave the needle inside the fold of the binding, and guide it along for about ⅜". Push the needle back out through the fold of the binding. Gently pull the thread taut, which will draw the binding down neatly against the back of the quilt.

5. Now that you've made the first stitch, you can begin to sew the blind stitch in a more fluid motion. Insert your needle into the backing and batting, right below the point where the thread is exiting the binding. Rock the needle back up through the quilt, very close to where you entered, and then push your needle into the fold of the binding fabric again. Travel along the fold ⅜", exit the binding, and then pull your thread through. Continue this stitch along the binding, giving your thread a good pull every four or five stitches to make sure the binding is secure against the backing.

6. As you sew the binding, be sure to miter the corners. The best method is to blind stitch almost to the corner, stopping at the stitching line where you originally sewed the binding strip to the quilt. Then finger press the diagonal fold in the binding **(Photo K)**.

K

L

7. Fold the next section of the binding over this one to create a mitered corner (**Photo L**). Sometimes you'll need to slip your needle into the miter fold and use it to flatten the fabric inside. Stitch the miter fold closed with a few blind stitches, and then push your needle back down between the mitered layers and back out at the spot where you'll continue sewing the binding.

CARING FOR YOUR QUILT

Quilts are meant to be used and loved, and they'll last for many years with a few simple care techniques.

Washing a Quilt: If you keep a quilt on your bed, and its contact with your skin (and household dirt) is minimal, then you shouldn't need to wash it more than once or twice a year. If a quilt is used frequently, it will likely need more frequent washing—but even with daily use, most quilts probably won't need washing more than once a month.

Washing a quilt repeatedly can put a lot of stress on the fabric and seams over time. If you have the option, wash your quilts in a front-loading washing machine or in a top-loading machine without an agitator. If you don't have access to these types of machines, maybe a friend or family member does. Wash your quilts in cold or warm water, and use a mild detergent that is free of fragrance and dye.

If your quilt is tie quilted, be sure not to use an agitator, as it can easily snag on the ties and pull them out. Tied quilts should probably be washed a bit less frequently in general than stitched quilts.

It's always best to dry a quilt by laying it flat, but not every household has enough space. You can also tumble-dry your quilt on a low-heat or no-heat setting, which shouldn't put too much stress on it.

All that said, please don't be afraid of damaging your quilts by washing them! There's no need to treat a quilt like a museum piece. You'll get the most enjoyment out of your quilts if you use them as much as possible.

Airing a Quilt: If your quilts see minimal use, then you can air them out a few times a year rather than submitting them to the stress of a washing machine. You don't have to have a proper clothesline; you can drape the quilt over a fence or a couple of patio chairs if need be.

Try to air your quilts on an overcast day, or if that's not feasible, at least limit the time the quilt is exposed to sunlight, given that too much sun can damage the fabrics and fade the colors. If you live in a sunny climate, air your quilts later in the evening when the sun begins to set. If you want to air a quilt and avoid the sun altogether, you can always tumble-dry it on a no-heat setting for about 30 minutes.

RESOURCES

Most of the supplies for the projects in this book are easy to find at your local quilting or fabric store. Here are places to find some of the less common supplies, plus a lot of books and websites we think you'll find interesting.

BOOKS ON QUILTING
Here are some of our favorites.

Beal, Susan. *Modern Log Cabin Quilting: 25 Simple Quilts and Patchwork Projects.* New York: Potter Craft, 2011.

Carlton, Alissa Haight, and Kristen Lejnieks. *Block Party: The Modern Quilting Bee—the Journey of 12 Women, 1 Blog, & 12 Improvisational Projects.* San Francisco: Stash Books, 2011.

Davis, Boo. *Dare to Be Square Quilting: A Block-by-Block Guide to Making Patchwork and Quilts.* New York: Potter Craft, 2010.

Gering, Jacquie, and Katie Pedersen. *Quilting Modern: Techniques and Projects for Improvisational Quilts.* Loveland: Interweave, 2012.

Hartmann, Elizabeth. *The Practical Guide to Patchwork: New Basics for the Modern Quiltmaker, 12 Quilt Projects.* Concord: C&T Publishing, 2010.

Linn, Don. *Free-Motion Machine Quilting.* Concord: C&T Publishing, 2011.

Ricucci, Tonya. *WordPlay Quilts: Easy Techniques from the Unruly Quilter.* Bothell: That Patchwork Place, 2010.

Walters, Angela. *Free-Motion Quilting with Angela Walters: Choose and Use Quilting Designs for Modern Quilts.* San Francisco: Stash Books, 2011.

BOOKS ON CREATIVITY
These books might help you think in a whole new way about how you create quilts.

Benton, Bridget. *The Creative Conversation: ArtMaking as Playful Prayer.* Portland: Eyes Aflame Publishing, 2011.

Kleon, Austin. *Steal Like an Artist: 10 Things Nobody Told You About Being Creative.* New York: Workman Publishing Company, 2012.

Messer, Mari. *Pencil Dancing: New Ways to Free Your Creative Spirit.* Cincinnati: Walking Stick Press, 2001.

FABRIC COMPANIES
These companies generously donated materials for the projects in this book. You can find their names attached to each project, and here's where to find them online.

Aurifil Threads: aurifil.com
Cloud 9 Fabrics (organic cottons): cloud9fabrics.com
Daisy Janie (organic cottons): daisyjanie.com
Moda: unitednotions.com
Riley Blake Designs: rileyblakedesigns.com
Westminster Fabrics: westminsterfabrics.com
Windham Fabrics: windhamfabrics.com

RESOURCE WEBSITES
Here are places to find tools and materials we mentioned in this book.

Acrylic templates: etsy.com/shop/TabSlot
Batting: warmcompany.com
Bernina sewing machines: berninausa.com
Binding clips: clover-usa.com
Color palette tools: colourlovers.com, kuler.adobe.com
Curve Master Presser Foot: justcurves.biz
Cutting mats, Dritz: dritz.com/brands/dritzcutting
Cutting mats, Omnigrid: dritz.com/brands/omnigrid
Dowel finials and caps: caseyswood.com
Erasable marking pens: clover-usa.com
Finger presser: clover-usa.com
FriXion pen: pilotpen us
Gingher scissors: gingher.us
Hera marking tool: clover-usa.com
Ink-jet fabric sheets: electricquilt.com, www.printedtreasures.com
Ink-jet treatment for cotton and silk yardage: cjenkinscompany.com
Oliso steam irons: oliso.com
Protect and Grip Thimble: clover-usa.com
Quilter's Dream Batting: quiltersdreambatting.com
Rotary cutters: fiskars.com

Rulers: olfaproducts.com
Ruler safety shield: olfaproducts.com
Vanishing Design Wall:
    vanishingdesignwall.com
Wonder Tape: dritz.com

QUILTERS FEATURED IN THIS BOOK

These talented folks agreed to be interviewed or provided quotes. Here's where to meet them online—go say hello!

Kay Bailey: fiberofherbeing.blogspot. com
Susan Beal: westcoastcrafty.com
Meryl Ann Butler:
    merylannbutler.com
Julie Cefalu: thecraftyquilter.com
Rashida Coleman-Hale:
    iheartlinen.typepad.com
Rachel Hauser: flickr.com/groups/ dogoodstitches
Katy Jones: fatquarterly.com, imagingermonkey.blogspot.co.uk
Monica Solorio-Snow:
    thehappyzombie.com

COMMUNITIES FOR QUILTERS

These websites offer online and offline places to connect with like-minded souls.

Fresh Modern Quilts Group: flickr. com/groups/freshmodernquilts
Quilt Blocks & Tops Group: flickr. com/groups/quiltblocks
Quilt guilds and quilt shows world-wide: quiltguilds.com
Quilting Bee Blocks:
    quiltingbeeblocks.com
Quilts and Quilting Group: flickr. com/groups/quilts/pool
The Modern Quilt Guild:
    themodernquiltguild.com

CHARITY QUILTING ORGANIZATIONS

Here are some places to contribute your quilting skills to meaningful causes.

do.Good Stitches: flickr.com/groups/ dogoodstitches
Project Linus: projectlinus.org
Quilts for Kids: quiltsforkids.org
Quilts for Quake Survivors: quiltsforquakesurvivors. wordpress.com
Threading Hope: threadinghope.com

QUILTING BLOGS AND WEBSITES

Here are some of our favorite reads and resources online.

Anna Maria Horner:
    annamariahorner.com
Fat Quarterly: fatquarterly.com
In Color Order:
    incolororder.blogspot.com
Missouri Star Quilt Company:
    missouriquiltco.com
Noodle Head: noodle-head.com
Oh, Fransson!: ohfransson.com
Poppyprint: poppyprintcreates. blogspot.com
Spoonflower (custom printed fabric): spoonflower.com
Trueup (a blog about fabric): trueup.net

PHOTOGRAPHERS IN THIS BOOK

Here are the people who created all the eye candy you enjoyed while reading.

Hanna Andersson, ihanna.nu
Kay Bailey,
    fiberofherbeing.blogspot.com
Sarah Costa,
    sarahcostaphotography.com
Nicke Cutler,
    kisskissquilt.blogspot.com
Pam and Kirby Harris,
    www.acep.com/harris_harris_ photographics.htm
Krista Hennebury,
    poppyprints.blogspot.com
Carol Porter,
    cloverusa.wordpress.com/tag/ carol-porter/
Heather Weston, heatherweston.com

TEMPLATES

Photocopy these templates onto card stock at full size, and then cut them out with scissors. For added stability, tape or glue the template to a second sheet of card stock before cutting it out. You can also have acrylic templates made from these diagrams; see the Resources section.

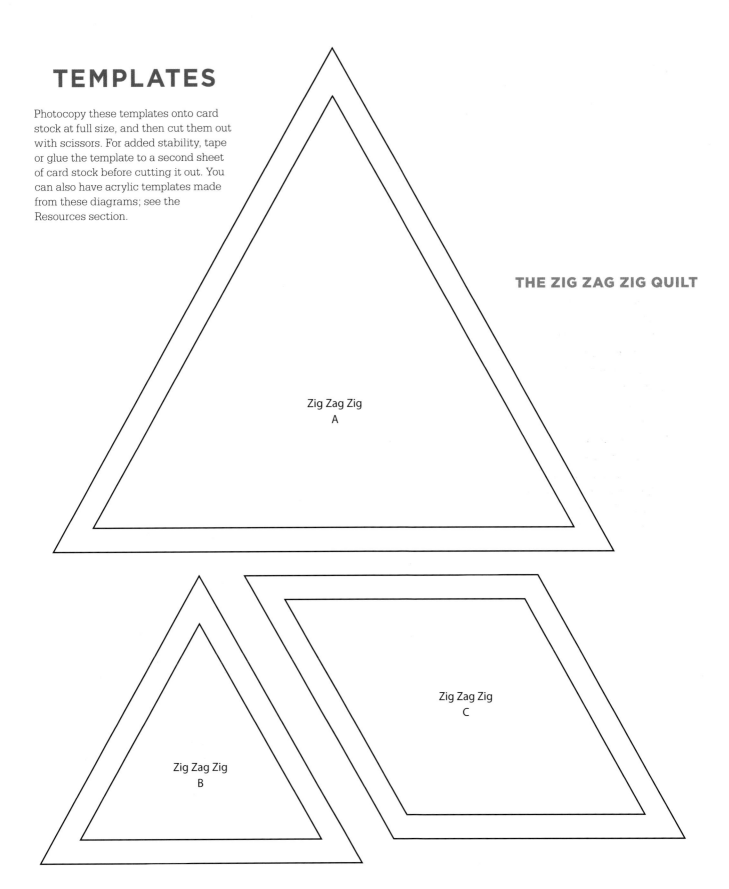

THE ZIG ZAG ZIG QUILT

Zig Zag Zig
A

Zig Zag Zig
B

Zig Zag Zig
C

THE PETAL PIE QUILT

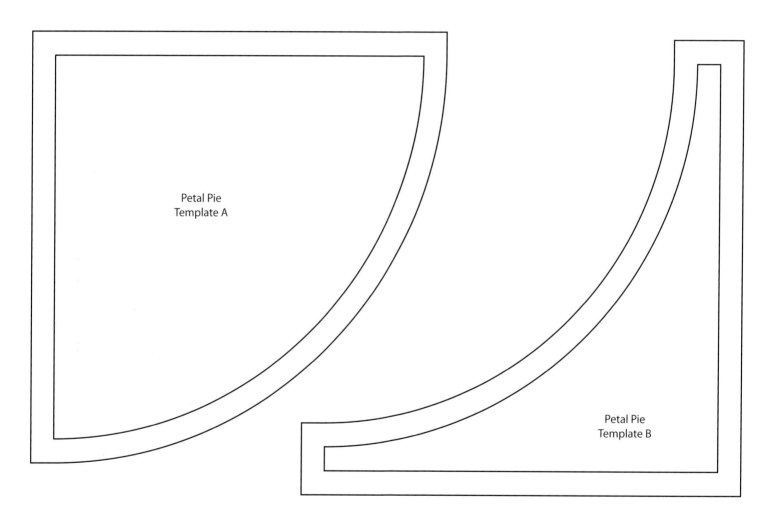

Petal Pie
Template A

Petal Pie
Template B

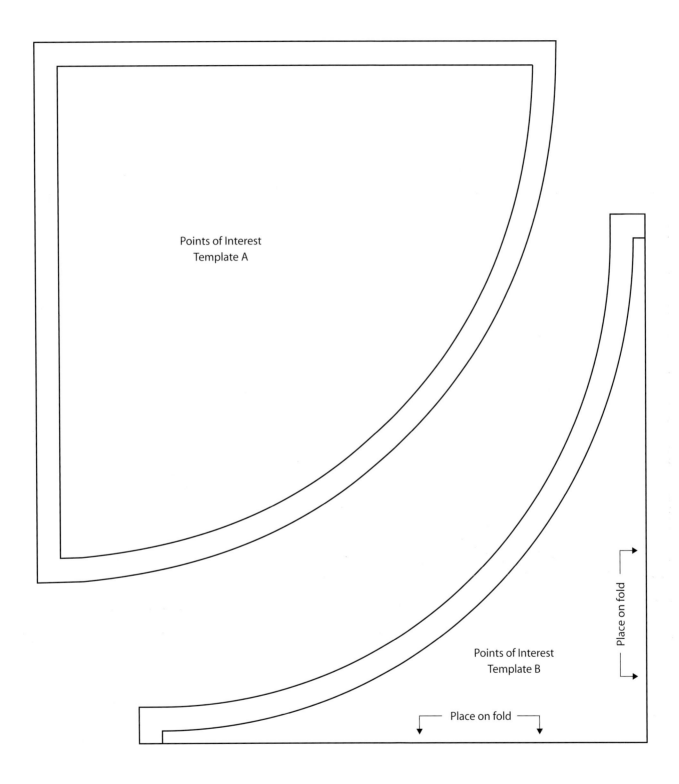

Points of Interest
Template A

Points of Interest
Template B

Place on fold

Place on fold

ACKNOWLEDGMENTS

Many kind people have contributed to the making of this book, and we're very grateful.

Kate McKean is an amazing agent who stewarded this project to completion with her usual smarts and good humor. We could not have made this book without her help.

Potter Craft produces lovely books, and we're thrilled to have had a chance to work with them.

Hanna Andersson, Cheryl Arkison, Kay Bailey, Susan Beal, Meryl Ann Butler, Julie Cefalu, Rashida Coleman-Hale, Jill Collins, Nicke Cutler, Allison Harris, Pam and Kirby Harris, Rachel Hauser, Lynne Heller, Katy Jones, Rachel Kerley, Tonya Ricucci, Annie Smith, and Monica Solario-Snow all provided bits of wisdom or beauty to this project. Thank you so much!

The Laid Back Ladies of the Block were kind enough to devote part of their summer retreat to sharing their story for this book. Thank you Carolyn Bennett, Kay Carrothers, Corki Duncan, Paula Erickson, Marta Estes, Laurie Giddings, Suzette Halferty, Beckie Hansen, Marion Harlan, Teresa Haskins, Carol Henry, Vicki Hesseltine, Betty Howland, Fran Ortmeyer, Erin Pakinas, Bev Payne, Carol Porter, Nadene Stephenson, Nancy Sweeney, and Sue Utt.

EXTRA THANKS . . .
FROM CHRISTINA

Aaron, my wonderfully supportive husband. Life was far from easy during the writing of this book, and you took it all in stride, allowing me to cross a life goal off my list.

Brice, Mommy can't tell you how wonderful you were during this process. When I said I really needed to work, you listened and kept yourself entertained. You were never far from my side during this whole process, and you always made sure to give me hugs and kisses and tell me you loved me, all through the day.

Mom, this never would have been possible without you. You never stopped trying to get me to sew when I was a kid, and were always ready with a "let's try" when I wanted to make something that wasn't what the pattern called for. Thank you for teaching me everything I know about sewing and for all of your help and support. I could not have finished in time without not only your help with Brice, but also with binding and hand quilting. Thank you from the bottom of my heart.

Liz Hutton, whoever thought thirteen years later we'd be the friends we are today? This book is as much yours as it is mine. You are always there for me, ready to give an encouraging word but also tell it like it is. Your honest opinion when I needed it (and sometimes didn't want to hear it) was invaluable. Thank you for all of your help in the making of the quilts and sewing of binding, and thank you for being the very best of friends always.

Sarah Costa, it's funny how crafting brought us together thirteen years ago and still brings us together today. We've gone from stamping together to sewing together to sharing our love of photography. Thank you so very much for taking the time to photograph the Tools and Techniques chapter. The photography is beautiful and I am so very excited to have one of my very dear friends be a part of this book.

Amanda Hall, you have been with this project from the start, giving me opinions on all of my designs, offering me an encouraging word when I needed it, and putting up with my absence for months on end. You are a true friend.

Jeni Baker, you too were there from the start, helping me with constructive criticism on designs and always helping me with color choices. You know my struggle with choosing fabric and colors, and have been a great help on several projects when I just couldn't decide what a stack of fabric needed to be perfect. Knowing you these last few years has made me more confident in my color choices.

Heather Lott, you saved me, excitedly taking on the construction of two very involved projects for me. You pieced Odds and Ends and Elevator Music flawlessly! Thank you, thank you, thank you! I'm so glad that our blogs brought us together, and that the Portland Modern Quilt Guild made us friends.

Many thanks to my mother-in-law and father-in-law, who excitedly looked forward to their Wednesday visits with Brice so I could have a few hours of peace to work. You know how much Brice loved his time with you, and I can never thank you enough.

And last, but far from least, a big thank-you to Diane for being the best coauthor I could ever ask for. You kept me organized and on task at the most crucial of times, and always pushed me to do better. I honestly could not have done this project without you. This was meant to be a book done together and I'm so happy that you decided to take this journey with me.

FROM DIANE

Katin Imes (the world's best partner), thank you for keeping the domestic machinery running, making sure I always had freshly roasted coffee, and convincing me to step away from the computer periodically.

Mom, thank you for the most excellent care packages of food you kept bringing me during the crunch weeks. They made a huge difference. Kirby, thank you so much for all that driving.

Christina, you are such a talented quilter, and a wonderful collaborator. It's been a real honor working with you. Can I still send you two thousand e-mails a week when this is over?

INDEX